AN INSPECTOR CALLS

BY J.B. PRIESTLEY

★

★

DRAMATISTS
PLAY SERVICE
INC.

An Inspector Calls was produced by Messrs. Courtney Burr and Lassor H. Grosberg at the Booth Theatre, New York City, on October 21, 1947, with the following cast:

ARTHUR BIRLING.................................Melville Cooper
GERALD CROFT..................................John Buckmaster
SHEILA BIRLING.......................................Rene Ray
SYBIL BIRLING......................................Doris Lloyd
EDNA ....Patricia Marmont
ERIC BIRLING......................................John Merivale
INSPECTOR GOOLE ....Thomas Mitchell

All three acts, which are continuous, take place in the dining-room of the Birlings' house in Brumley, an industrial city in the North Midlands.

It is an evening in Spring, 1912.

The Dramatists Play Service wishes to thank Mr. Al Checco, Stage Manager of the New York production, for his courtesy in preparing the scene design used in this text.

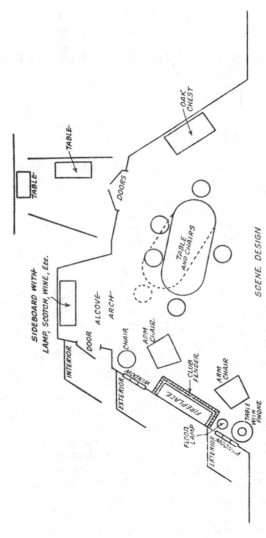

SCENE DESIGN

"AN INSPECTOR CALLS"

Notice that center table is re-drawn with a dotted line. The solidly drawn diagram shows the table for Act I only. There is a good deal of business at the table during that act. After it, the table is just in the way as set. By moving it up a few feet as indicated, the director in Acts II and III, may use the upstage arm chair (which is not used in Act I, because of sight lines). It is suggested that a round table be used.

4

AN INSPECTOR CALLS

ACT I

SCENE: *Dining-room of a fairly large suburban house, belonging to a fairly prosperous manufacturer. It is a solidly built room, with good solid furniture of the period. Upstage right there is an alcove with a heavy sideboard. A door from the alcove leads to the kitchen. Upstage left is a large double door used almost exclusively. A fireplace is along the right wall with a curtained window on either side. There are two leather armchairs on either side of the fireplace and down stage from it an ornate floor lamp and a small table with telephone. A little upstage of center is a solid but not too large dining room table with solid set of dining room chairs around it. A few imposing but tasteless pictures and engravings. The general effect is substantial and comfortable and old-fashioned but not cozy and homelike.*

AT RISE OF CURTAIN: *The four* BIRLINGS *and* GERALD *are seated at table, with* ARTHUR BIRLING *at one end, his wife at the other,* ERIC BIRLING *downstage, and* SHEILA *and* GERALD CROFT *seated upstage.* EDNA, *a neatly dressed parlor maid, in her late twenties, is just clearing table which has no cloth, of dessert plates, champagne glasses and champagne bottle, taking them to sideboard, then going back to table with decanter of port. Port glasses are already on table. All five are in evening dress of the period, the men in tails and white ties.* ARTHUR BIRLING *is a heavy-looking, rather portentous man in his middle fifties, with fairly easy manners but rather provincial in his speech. His wife is about fifty, a rather cold woman and her husband's*

5

social superior. SHEILA *is a pretty girl in her early twenties, very pleased with life and rather excited.* GERALD CROFT *is an attractive chap about thirty, rather too manly to be a dandy, but very much the easy well-bred young-man-about-town.* ERIC *is in his middle twenties, not quite at ease, half shy, half assertive. At the moment they have all had a good dinner, are celebrating a special occasion, and are pleased with themselves.*

BIRLING. Thank you, Edna. That's right. (*Pushes port toward* ERIC. EDNA *crosses to* U. *sideboard.*) You ought to like this port, Gerald. As a matter of fact, Finchley assured me it's exactly the same port your father gets from him.

GERALD. Then it'll be all right. The governor prides himself on being a good judge of port. I don't pretend to know much about it. (EDNA *crosses down to table.*)

SHEILA. (*Gaily, possessively.*) I should jolly well think so, Gerald. I'd hate you to know all about port—like one of these purple-faced old men. (EDNA *crosses to sideboard.*)

BIRLING. Here, I'm not a purple-faced old man.

SHEILA. No, not yet. But then you don't know all about port—do you?

BIRLING. (*Noticing that his wife,* SYBIL, *has not taken any.*) Now then, Sybil, you must take a little tonight. Special occasion, y'know, eh?

SHEILA. Yes, go on, Mummy. You must drink our health. (EDNA *goes to table.*)

MRS. BIRLING. (*Smiling.*) Very well, then. Just a little, thank you. (*To* EDNA, *who is about to go with tray.*) All right, Edna. I'll ring from the drawing-room when we want coffee. Probably in about half an hour. (EDNA *crosses to kitchen door.*)

EDNA. (*Going.*) Yes, Ma'am. (EDNA *goes out. They now have all the glasses filled.* BIRLING *beams at them and clearly relaxes.*)

BIRLING. Well, well—this is very nice. Very nice. Good dinner too, Sybil. Tell Cook from me.

GERALD. (*Politely.*) Absolutely first-class.

MRS. BIRLING. (*Reproachfully.*) Arthur, you're not supposed to say such things ——

6

BIRLING. Oh—come, come—I'm treating Gerald like one of the family. And I'm sure he won't object.

SHEILA. (*With mock aggressiveness.*) Go on, Gerald—just you object!

GERALD. (*Smiling.*) Wouldn't dream of it. In fact, I insist upon being one of the family now. I've been trying long enough, haven't I? (*As* SHEILA *does not reply, with more insistence.*) Haven't I? You know I have.

MRS. BIRLING. (*Smiling.*) Of course she does.

SHEILA. (*Half serious, half playful.*) Yes—except for all last summer when you never came near me, and I wondered what had happened to you.

GERALD. And I've told you—I was awfully busy at the works all that time.

SHEILA. (*Same tone as before.*) Yes, that's what *you* say.

MRS. BIRLING. Now, Sheila, don't tease him. When you're married you'll realize that men with important work to do sometimes have to spend nearly all their time and energy on their business. You'll have to get used to that, just as I had. Isn't that so, Arthur?

BIRLING. Quite, quite.

SHEILA. I don't believe I will. (*Half playful, half serious. To* GERALD.) So you be careful.

GERALD. Oh—I will, I will. (ERIC *suddenly guffaws. Rises, crosses to fender. His parents look at him.*)

SHEILA. (*Severely.*) Now—what's the joke?

ERIC. I don't know—I just suddenly felt I had to laugh.

SHEILA. You're squiffy.

ERIC. I'm not.

MRS. BIRLING. What an expression, Sheila! Really, the things you girls pick up these days!

ERIC. (*Sits on fender.*) If you think that's the best she can do ——

SHEILA. Don't be an ass, Eric.

MRS. BIRLING. Now stop it, you two. Arthur, what about this famous toast of yours?

BIRLING. (*Rising.*) Yes, of course. (*Clears his throat.*) Well, Gerald, I know you agreed that we should only have this quiet little family party. It's a pity Sir George and—er—Lady Croft can't be with us, but they're abroad and so it can't be helped. As I told you, they sent me a very nice cable—couldn't be nicer. I'm not sorry that we're celebrating quietly like this ——

7

MRS. BIRLING. Much nicer, really.

GERALD. I quite agree.

BIRLING. So do I, but it makes speech-making more difficult.

ERIC. (*Not too rudely.*) Well, don't do any.

BIRLING. What?

ERIC. Don't do any.

BIRLING. Oh yes, I will. This is one of the happiest nights of my life. And one day, I hope, Eric, when you've a daughter of your own, you'll understand why. Gerald, I'm going to tell you frankly, without any pretenses, that your engagement to Sheila means a tremendous lot to me. She'll make you happy. I'm sure you'll make her happy. You're just the kind of son-in-law I've always wanted. Your father and I have been friendly rivals in business for some time now—though Crofts Limited are both older and bigger than Birling and Company—and now you've brought us together, and perhaps we may look forward to the time when Crofts and Birlings are no longer competing but are working together—for lower costs and higher prices.

GERALD. Hear, hear! And I think my father would agree to that, too.

MRS. BIRLING. Now, Arthur, I don't think you ought to talk business on an occasion like this.

SHEILA. Neither do I. All wrong.

BIRLING. Quite so, I agree with you. I only mentioned it in passing. What I did want to say was—that Sheila's a lucky girl—and, Gerald, I think you're a pretty fortunate young man, too.

GERALD. I know I am—just this once anyhow.

BIRLING. (*Rises, raising his glass.*) So here's wishing the pair of you—the very best that life can bring. Gerald and Sheila!

ERIC. All the best.

MRS. BIRLING. (*Raising her glass, smiling.*) Yes, Gerald.

ERIC. (*Rather noisily.*) All the best! She's got a nasty temper sometimes—but she's not bad really. Good old Sheila!

MRS. BIRLING. Yes, Sheila, darling. (*Rises, as does* ERIC.) Our congratulations and very best wishes!

GERALD. Thank you. (ALL *sit.*)

SHEILA. Chump! I can't drink to this, can I? When do I drink?

GERALD. You can drink to me.

SHEILA. (*Quiet and serious now.*) All right, then. I drink to you. (*Rises. For a moment they look at each other.*)

GERALD. (*Quietly. Rising.*) Thank you. And I drink to you—and hope I can make you as happy as you deserve to be.

SHEILA. (*Pause. Trying to be light and easy. Sits.*) You be careful—or I'll start weeping.

GERALD. (*Smiling. Sitting.*) Well, perhaps this will help to stop it. (*Produces a ring case.*)

SHEILA. (*Excited.*) Oh—Gerald—you've got it—is it the one you wanted me to have?

GERALD. (*Giving case to her.*) Yes—the very one.

SHEILA. (*Taking out ring.*) Oh—it's wonderful! Look— Mummy —— (*Crosses to* MRS. BIRLING.) Isn't it a beauty? Oh— darling —— (*Crosses to below* MRS. BIRLING. *Kisses* GERALD *hastily.*)

ERIC. Steady, old girl! The buffs.

SHEILA. (*Who has put ring on, admiringly.*) I think it's perfect. Now I really feel engaged.

MRS. BIRLING. So you ought, darling. It's a lovely ring. Be careful with it.

SHEILA. (*Crossing down* R., ERIC *going to her.*) Careful! I'll never let it go out of my sight for an instant. Look, Eric.

MRS. BIRLING. (*Smiling.*) Well, it came just at the right moment. That was clever of you, Gerald. Now, Arthur, if you've no more to say, I think Sheila and I had better go into the drawing-room and leave you men —— (*She and* GERALD *rise.*)

BIRLING. (*Rather heavily.*) I just want to say this. (GERALD *and* MRS. BIRLING *sit.* BIRLING, *noticing that* SHEILA *is still admiring her ring.*) Are you listening, Sheila? This concerns you, too.

SHEILA. I'm sorry, Daddy. Actually, I was listening. (*Crosses to her chair and sits. She looks attentive, as they all do.* ERIC *sits down* R.)

BIRLING. (*Holding them a moment before continuing. Tries to cross legs through speech.*) I'm delighted about this engagement and I hope it won't be too long before you're married. And I want to say this. There's a good deal of silly talk about these days—but—and I speak as a hard-headed business man, who has to take risks and know what he's about—I say, you can ignore all this silly pessimistic talk. When you marry, you'll be marrying at a very good time. Yes, a very good time—and soon it'll be an even better time.

GERALD. I believe you're right, sir.

ERIC. What about war?

BIRLING. What? Don't interrupt, Eric. I was coming to that. Just because the Kaiser makes a speech or two, or a few German officers have too much to drink and begin talking nonsense, you'll hear some people say that war's inevitable. And to that I say—fiddlesticks! The Germans don't want war. Nobody wants war, except some half-civilized folks in the Balkans. And why? There's too much at stake these days. Everything to lose and nothing to gain by war.

ERIC. Yes, I know—but still ——

BIRLING. Just let me finish, Eric. You've a lot to learn yet. And I'm talking as a hard-headed, practical man of business. And I say there isn't a chance of war. The world's developing so fast that it'll make war impossible. Look at the progress we're making. In a year or two we'll have aeroplanes that will be able to go anywhere. And look at the way the automobile's making headway—bigger and faster all the time. And then ships. Why, a friend of mine went over this new liner last week—forty-six thousand eight hundred tons—forty-six thousand eight hundred tons—New York in five days—and every luxury—and unsinkable, absolutely unsinkable. That's what you've got to keep your eye on, facts like that, progress like that—and not a few German officers talking nonsense and a few scaremongers here making a fuss about nothing. Now you three young people, listen to this—and remember what I'm telling you now. In twenty or thirty years' time—let's say, in the forties—you may be giving a little party like this—your son or daughter might be getting engaged—and I tell you, by that time you'll be living in a world that'll have forgotten all these Capital versus Labor agitations and all these silly little war scares. There'll be peace and prosperity and rapid progress everywhere—except of course in Russia, which will always be behind-hand, naturally. (MRS. BIRLING *shows signs of interrupting.*)

MRS. BIRLING. Yes, dear—I know.

BIRLING. Yes, my dear, I know—I'm talking too much. But we can't let these Bernard Shaws and H. G. Wellses do all the talking. We hard-headed practical businessmen must say something sometime. And we don't guess—we've had experience—and we *know.*

MRS. BIRLING. (*Rising. Others rise.* BIRLING *to fireplace for cigars.*)
Yes, of course, dear. Well—don't keep Gerald in here too long.
Eric—(*To door.*)—I want you a minute. (*She and* SHEILA *and*
ERIC, *whistling "Rule Britannia" goes out* L. GERALD *opens door for
them.* BIRLING *and* GERALD *sit down again.*[1])
BIRLING. Cigar?
GERALD. No, thanks. I can't really enjoy them.
BIRLING. (*Crossing and taking one himself.*) Ah, you don't know
what you're missing. I like a good cigar. (*Indicating decanter.*)
Help yourself to the port. (BIRLING *lights his cigar and* GERALD,
*who has lit a cigarette, helps himself to port, then pushes de-
canter to* BIRLING. GERALD *crosses to* U. R. *chair, sits.*)
GERALD. Thanks.
BIRLING. (*Confidentially.*) By the way, there's something I'd like
to mention—in strict confidence—while we're by ourselves. I have
an idea that your mother—Lady Croft—while she doesn't object
to my girl—feels you might have done better for yourself so-
cially —— (GERALD, *rather embarrassed, begins to murmur some
dissent, but* BIRLING *checks him.*) No, Gerald, that's all right.
Don't blame her. She comes from an old county family—landed
people and so forth—and so it's only natural. But what I wanted
to say is—there's a fair chance that I might find my way into
the next Honors List. Just a knighthood, of course.
GERALD. Oh—I say—congratulations!
BIRLING. (*At fireplace.*) Thanks. But it's a bit too early for that.
So don't say anything. But I've had a hint or two. You see, I
was Lord Mayor here two years ago when Royalty visited us.
And I've always been regarded as a sound, useful party man.
So—well—I gather there's a very good chance of a knighthood—so
long as we behave ourselves, don't get into the police court or
start a scandal—eh? (*Laughs complacently.*)
GERALD. (*Laughs.*) You seem to be a very well-behaved family
to me ——
BIRLING. We think we are ——
GERALD. So if that's the only obstacle, sir, I think you might as
well accept my congratulations now.
BIRLING. Thank you. No, no, I couldn't do that. And don't say
anything yet.

---

[1] All exits and entrances hereafter are through c. door.

GERALD. I say, could I say something to my mother about this? I know she'd be delighted.

BIRLING. Well, when she comes back, you might drop a hint to her. (*They both laugh.* ERIC *enters.*)

ERIC. What's up? Started telling your stories yet?

BIRLING. No. Want another glass of port? (*Sits* R. *chair.*)

ERIC. (*Sitting down.*) Yes, please. (*Takes decanter and helps himself.*) Mother says we mustn't stay too long. But I don't think it matters. I left 'em talking about clothes again. You'd think a girl had never had any clothes before she gets married. Women are potty about 'em. (*Sits* L. *chair.*)

BIRLING. Yes, but you've got to remember, my boy, that clothes mean something quite different to a woman. Not just something to wear—and not only something to make 'em look prettier—but —well, a sort of sign or token of their self-respect.

GERALD. That's true.

ERIC. (*Eagerly.*) Yes, I remember —— (*But he checks himself.*)

BIRLING. Well, what do you remember?

ERIC. (*Confused.*) Nothing.

BIRLING. Nothing?

GERALD. (*Amused.*) Sounds a bit fishy to me.

BIRLING. (*Taking it in same manner.*) Yes, you don't know what some of these boys get up to nowadays. More money to spend and time to spare than I had when I was Eric's age. They worked us hard in those days and kept us short of cash. Though even then—we broke out and had a bit of fun sometimes.

GERALD. I'll bet you did.

BIRLING. (*Solemnly.*) But this is the point. I don't want to lecture you two young fellows again. But what so many of you don't seem to understand now when things are so much easier, is that a man has to make his own way—has to look after himself—and his family, too, of course, when he has one—and so long as he does that he won't come to much harm. But the way some of these cranks talk and write now, you'd think everybody has to look after everybody else, as if we were all mixed up together like bees in a hive—a man has to mind his own business and look after himself and his own—and —— (*We hear sharp ring of a front doorbell.* BIRLING *stops to listen.*)

ERIC. Somebody at the front door.

BIRLING. All right, Eric. Edna'll answer it. Well, have another glass of port, Gerald—and then we'll join the ladies. That'll stop me giving you good advice.

ERIC. Yes, you've piled it on a bit tonight, Father.

BIRLING. Special occasion. And feeling contented, for once, I wanted you to have the benefit of my experience. (EDNA *enters, crosses* U. L. *to table.*)

EDNA. Please, sir.

BIRLING. Yes?

EDNA. An inspector's called.

LIRLING. An inspector? What kind of inspector?

EDNA. A police inspector. He says his name's Inspector Goole.

BIRLING. Don't know him. Does he want to see me?

EDNA. Yes, sir. He says it's important.

BIRLING. All right, Edna. Show him in here. (EDNA *goes out.*) It may be something about a warrant. I'm still on the Bench.

GERALD. (*Lightly.*) Eric's probably been up to something. (*Nodding confidentially to* BIRLING.) And that would be awkward, wouldn't it?

BIRLING. (*Humorously.*) Very.

ERIC. (*Who is uneasy, sharply.*) Here, what do you mean?

GERALD. (*Lightly.*) Only something we were talking about before you came in. A joke really.

ERIC. (*Still uneasy.*) Well, I don't think it's very funny.

BIRLING. (*Sharply, staring at him.*) What's the matter with you?

ERIC. (*Defiantly.*) Nothing. (EDNA *opens door and announces.*)

EDNA. Inspector Goole. (*The* INSPECTOR *enters, and* EDNA *goes out* L., *crosing door. The* INSPECTOR *need not be a big man, but he creates at once an impression of massiveness, solidity, and purposefulness. He is a man in his fifties, dressed in a plain darkish suit of the period. He speaks carefully, weightily, and has a disconcerting habit of looking hard at the person he addresses before actually speaking.*)

INSPECTOR. Mr. Birling?

BIRLING. (*Rises.*) Good evening, Inspector. You're new, aren't you?

INSPECTOR. (*Crosses to him.*) Yes, sir. Only recently transferred.

BIRLING. I thought you must be. I was an alderman for years—and Lord Mayor two years ago—and I'm still on the Bench—so I know the Brumley police officers pretty well—and I thought I'd never seen you before.

INSPECTOR. Quite so.

BIRLING. Yes. Sit down, Inspector.

INSPECTOR. (*Crossing down* R., *sitting.*) Thank you, sir.

BIRLING. Have a glass of port—or a little whiskey.

INSPECTOR. No, thank you, Mr. Birling. I'm on duty.

BIRLING. (*Shifting chair.*) Well, what can I do for you? Some trouble about a warrant?

INSPECTOR. No, Mr. Birling.

BIRLING. (*After a pause, with a touch of impatience.*) Well, what is it then?

INSPECTOR. I'd like some information, if you don't mind, Mr. Birling. Two hours ago a young woman died in the Infirmary. She'd been taken there this afternoon because she'd swallowed a lot of strong disinfectant. Burnt her inside out, of course.

ERIC. (*Involuntarily.*) My God!

INSPECTOR. Yes, she was in great agony. They did everything they could for her at the Infirmary, but she died. Suicide, of course.

BIRLING. (*Rather impatiently.*) Yes, yes. Horrible business. (*Drinks.*) But I don't understand why you should come here, Inspector ——?

INSPECTOR. (*Cutting through, massively.*) I've been round to the room she had, and she'd left a letter there and a sort of diary. Like a lot of these young women who get into various kinds of trouble, she'd used more than one name. But her original name— her real name—was Eva Smith.

BIRLING. (*Thoughtfully.*) Eva Smith?

INSPECTOR. Do you remember her, Mr. Birling?

BIRLING. (*Slowly.*) No —— I seem to remember hearing that name—Eva Smith—somewhere. But it doesn't convey anything to me. And I don't see where I come into this.

INSPECTOR. She was employed in your works at one time.

BIRLING. (*Crossing over toward fireplace.*) Oh—that's it, is it? Well, we've several hundred young women there, y'know, and they keep changing.

INSPECTOR. This young woman, Eva Smith, was a bit out of the ordinary. I found a photograph of her in her lodgings. (*Rises.*) Perhaps you'd remember her from that? (BIRLING *crosses to* D. R. *lamp.* INSPECTOR *rises and walks behind table to* BIRLING. ERIC *and* GERALD *rise.* GERALD *crosses to* D. R. INSPECTOR *stops him* D. R. C. INSPECTOR *takes photograph, about post card size, out of pocket and goes to* BIRLING, *who is now standing. Both* GERALD

14

and ERIC *rise to have a look at photograph, but* INSPECTOR *interposes himself between them and photograph. They are surprised and rather annoyed.* BIRLING *stares hard, and with recognition, at photograph, which* INSPECTOR *then replaces in his pocket.*)

GERALD. (*Showing annoyance.*) Any particular reason why I shouldn't see this girl's photograph, Inspector?

INSPECTOR. (*Coolly, looking hard at him.*) There might be.

ERIC. And the same applies to me, I suppose?

INSPECTOR. Yes.

GERALD. I can't imagine what it could be. (*Crosses to his chair.*)

ERIC. Neither can I. (*Sits* L. *chair.*)

BIRLING. And I must say I agree with them, Inspector.

INSPECTOR. It's the way I like to go to work. One person and one line of inquiry at a time. Otherwise, there's a muddle.

BIRLING. I see. (*Crosses to* R. *chair. Moves restlessly, then turns.*) I think you've had enough of that port, Eric! (ERIC *turns a chair or two to face downstage. This, with the two armchairs, now gives the place almost the appearance of a sitting-room.* INSPECTOR *is watching* BIRLING, *and now* BIRLING *notices him.*)

INSEPCTOR. I think you remember Eva Smith now, don't you, Mr. Birling?   •

BIRLING. Yes, I do. She was one of my employees, and then I discharged her.

ERIC. Is that why she committed suicide? When was this, Father?

BIRLING. (*Crossing to* R. *chair.*) Just keep quiet, Eric, and don't get excited. This girl left us nearly two years ago. Let me see—it must have been in the early autumn of 1910.

INSPECTOR. Yes. End of September, 1910.

BIRLING. That's right.

GERALD. Look here, sir. Wouldn't you rather I was out of this? (*Rises.*)

BIRLING. I don't mind your being here, Gerald. And I'm sure you've no objection, have you, Inspector? Perhaps I ought to explain first that this is Mr. Gerald Croft—son of Sir George Croft —you know, Crofts Limited.

INSPECTOR. Mr. Gerald Croft?

BIRLING. (*Sits* R. *chair.*) Yes. Incidentally, we've been modestly celebrating his engagement to my daughter Sheila.

INSPECTOR. I see. Mr. Croft is going to marry Miss Sheila Birling?

GERALD. (*Smiling.*) I hope so.

INSPECTOR. (*Gravely.*) Then I'd prefer you to stay.

GERALD. (*Surprised.*) Oh—all right.

BIRLING. (*Somewhat impatiently.*) Look—there's nothing mysterious—about this business—at least not so far as I'm concerned. It's a perfectly straightforward case, and as it happened more than eighteen months ago—nearly two years ago—obviously it has nothing whatever to do with the wretched girl's suicide. Eh, Inspector?

INSPECTOR. No, sir. I can't agree with you there.

BIRLING. Why not?

INSPECTOR. Because what happened to her then may have determined what happened to her afterwards, and what happened to her afterwards may have driven her to suicide. A chain of events.

BIRLING. Oh, well—put like that, there's something in what you say. Still, I can't accept any responsibility. If we are all responsible for everything that happened to everybody we'd had anything to do with, it would be very awkward, wouldn't it?

INSPECTOR. Very awkward.

BIRLING. We'd all be in an impossible position, wouldn't we?

ERIC. By Jove, yes. And as you were saying, Dad, a man has to look after himself ——

BIRLING. Yes, well, we needn't go into all that.

INSPECTOR. Go into what?

BIRLING. Oh—just before you came—I'd been giving (*Pours port.*) these young men a little good advice. Now—about this girl, Eva Smith. I remember her quite well now. She was a lively, good-looking girl—country-bred, I fancy—and she'd been working in one of our machine shops for over a year. A good worker, too. In fact, the foreman there told me he was ready to promote her into what we called a leading operator—head of a small group of girls. But after they came back from their holidays that August, they were all rather restless, and they suddenly decided to ask for more money. They were averaging about twenty-two shillings, which was neither more nor less than is paid generally in our industry. They wanted the rates raised so that they could average about twenty-five shillings a week. I refused, of course.

INSPECTOR. Why?

BIRLING. (*Surprised.*) What! Did you say " Why " ?

INSPECTOR. Yes. Why did you refuse?

BIRLING. Well, Inspector, I don't see that it's any concern of yours how I choose to run my business. Is it now?

INSPECTOR. It might be, you know.

BIRLING. I don't like that tone.

INSPECTOR. I'm sorry. But you asked me a question.

BIRLING. And you asked me a question too, before that, a quite unnecessary question, too.

INSPECTOR. It's my duty to ask questions.

BIRLING. Well, it's my duty to keep labor costs down, (*Turns to chair.*) and if I'd agreed to this demand for a new rate we'd have added about twelve per cent to our labor costs. Does that satisfy you? So I refused. Said I couldn't consider it. We were paying the usual rates and if they didn't like those rates, they could go and work somewhere else. It's a free country, I told them. (*Sits chair.*)

ERIC. It isn't if you can't go and work somewhere else.

INSPECTOR. Quite so.

BIRLING. (*To* ERIC.) Look—just you keep out of this. You hadn't even started in the works when this happened. So they went on strike. That didn't last long, of course.

GERALD. Not if it was just after the summer holidays. They'd be all broke—if I know them.

BIRLING. Right, Gerald. They mostly were. And so was the strike, after a week or two. Pitiful affair. Well, we forgave them, we let them all come back—at the old rates—except the four or five ringleaders, who'd started the trouble. I went down myself and told them to clear out. And this girl, Eva Smith, was one of them. She'd had a lot to say, I remember—far too much—so she had to go.

GERALD. You couldn't really have done anything else.

ERIC. He could. He could have kept her on instead of throwing her out. I call it tough luck.

BIRLING. Rubbish! If you don't come down sharply on some ot these people, they'd soon be asking for the earth.

GERALD. I should say so!

INSPECTOR. They might. But after all it's better to ask for the earth than to take it.

BIRLING. (*Staring at* INSPECTOR. *Rises, crosses* D. R.) What did you say your name was, Inspector?

17

INSPECTOR. Goole. (*Sits* D. R.)

BIRLING. (*Rises, crosses to him. Then to fender before fireplace.* INSPECTOR *sits.*) Goole, how do you get on with our Chief Constable? Colonel Roberts?

INSPECTOR. I don't see much of him. (*Sits* D. R.)

BIRLING. Perhaps I ought to warn you that he's an old friend of mine, and that I see him fairly frequently. We play golf together sometimes up at the West Brumley.

INSPECTOR. (*Drily.*) I don't play golf.

BIRLING. I didn't suppose you did.

ERIC. (*Bursting out.*) Well, I think it's a dam' shame.

INSPECTOR. (*Going* L.) No, I've never wanted to play.

ERIC. No, I mean about this girl—Eva Smith. Why shouldn't they try for higher wages? We try for the highest possible prices. And I don't see why she should have been sacked just because she'd a bit more spirit than the others. You said yourself she was a good worker. I'd have let her stay.

BIRLING. (*Rather angrily. Steps toward* ERIC.) Unless you brighten your ideas, you'll never be in a position to let anybody stay or to tell anybody to go. It's about time you learnt to face a few responsibilities. That's something this public school and Varsity life you've had doesn't seem to have taught.

ERIC. (*Sulkily.*) Well, we don't need to tell the Inspector all about that, do we?

BIRLING. (*Crossing to* INSPECTOR.) I don't see we need to tell the Inspector anything more. In fact, (*At fender.*) there's nothing I can tell him. I told the girl to clear out, and she went. That's the last I heard of her. Have you any idea what happened to her after that? Get into trouble? Go on the streets?

INSPECTOR. (*Rather slowly.*) No, she didn't exactly go on the streets. (SHEILA *has now entered, and crosses to* BIRLING. INSPECTOR *and* GERALD *rise.*)

SHEILA. (*Gaily.*) What's this about streets? (*Noticing* INSPECTOR.) Oh—sorry. I didn't know. Mummy sent me in to ask you why you didn't come along to the drawing-room?

BIRLING. We shall be along in a minute now. Just finishing.

INSPECTOR. I'm afraid not.

BIRLING. (*Abruptly.*) There's nothing else, y'know. I've just told you that.

SHEILA. What's all this about?

BIRLING. Nothing to do with you, Sheila. Run along. (*She starts to go.*)

INSPECTOR. No, wait a minute, Miss Birling. (SHEILA *drifts back to* D. L. C.)

BIRLING. (*Angrily, crossing to him.*) Look here, Inspector, I consider this uncalled-for and officious. I've half a mind to report you. I've told you all I know—and it doesn't seem to me very important—and now there isn't the slightest reason why my daughter should be dragged into this unpleasant business.

SHEILA. (*Coming further in.*) What business? What's happening?

INSPECTOR. (*Impressively.*) I'm a police inspector, Miss Birling. This afternoon a young woman drank some disinfectant, and died, after several hours of agony, tonight in the Infirmary.

SHEILA. Oh—how horrible! Was it an accident?

INSPECTOR. No. She wanted to end her life. She felt she couldn't go on any longer.

BIRLING. Well, don't tell me that's because I discharged her from my employment nearly two years ago!

ERIC. That might have started it.

SHEILA. Did you, Dad? (*Sits* R. *chair.*)

BIRLING. Yes. The girl had been causing trouble in the works. I was quite justified.

GERALD. Yes, I think you were. I know we'd have done the same thing. Don't look like that, Sheila.

SHEILA. (*Rather distressed.*) Sorry! It's just that I can't help thinking about this girl—destroying herself so horribly—and I've been so happy tonight. Oh, I wish he hadn't told me. What was she like? Quite young?

INSPECTOR. Yes. Twenty-four.

SHEILA. Pretty?

INSPECTOR. She wasn't pretty when I saw her today, but she had been pretty—very pretty.

BIRLING. That's enough of that.

GERALD. And I don't really see that this inquiry gets you anywhere, Inspector. It's what happened to her since she left Mr. Birling's works that is important.

BIRLING. Obviously. I suggested that some time ago. (*Crossing to front of fireplace.*)

GERALD. And we can't help you there, because we don't know. (*Sits.*)

19

INSPECTOR. (*Slowly.*) Are you sure you don't know? (*He looks at* GERALD, *then at* ERIC, *then at* SHEILA.)

BIRLING. And are you suggesting now that one of them knows something about this girl? (ERIC *and* GERALD *rise.* ERIC *goes* D. L.)

INSPECTOR. Yes.

BIRLING. You didn't come here just to see me then? (*Crosses* D. C., *looking at* GERALD, *and goes back* R. C.)

INSPECTOR. No. (*Other four exchange bewildered and perturbed glances. Pause.*)

BIRLING. (*Crossing* D. C., *looking at* ERIC, *then back to* INSPECTOR —*pats shoulder. With marked change of tone.*) Well, of course, if I'd known that earlier, I wouldn't have called you officious and talked about reporting you. You understand that, don't you, Inspector? I thought that—for some reason best known to yourself—you were making the most of this tiny bit of information I could give you. I'm sorry. This makes a difference. (*To fireplace.*) You sure of your facts?

INSPECTOR. Some of them—yes.

BIRLING. They don't seem to amount to very much, though. Do they?

INSPECTOR. The girl's dead, though.

SHEILA. What do you mean by saying that? You talk as if we were responsible ——

BIRLING. (*Cutting in.*) Just a minute, Sheila. Now, Inspector, (*Crossing to him.*) perhaps you and I had better go and talk this over quietly in a corner ——

SHEILA. (*Cutting in.*) Why should you? He's finished with you. He says it's one of us now.

BIRLING. (*Crossing to her.*) Yes, and I'm trying to settle it sensibly for you.

GERALD. (*Sits.*) Well, there's nothing to settle as far as I'm concerned. I've never known an Eva Smith.

ERIC. (*Crossing to* L. *chair, sits.*) Neither have I.

SHEILA. Was that her name? Eva Smith?

GERALD. Yes.

SHEILA. (BIRLING *to fender.*) Never heard it before.

GERALD. So where are you now, Inspector?

INSPECTOR. Where I was before, Mr. Croft. I told you—that like a lot of these young women, she'd used more than one name. She was still Eva Smith when Mr. Birling sacked her—for wanting twenty-five shillings a week instead of twenty-two. But after that she stopped being Eva Smith. Perhaps she'd had enough of it.

ERIC. Can't blame her.

SHEILA. (*To* BIRLING.) I think it was a mean thing to do. Perhaps that spoilt everything for her.

BIRLING. Rubbish! (*To* INSPECTOR.) Do you happen to know what became of her after she left my employment?

INSPECTOR. Yes. She was out of work for the next two months. Both her parents were dead so that she'd no home to go back to. And she hadn't been able to save much out of what Birling and Company had paid her. So after two months, with no work, no money coming in, and living in lodgings, with no relatives to help her, few friends, lonely, half-starved, she was feeling desperate.

SHEILA. (*Warmly.*) I should think so. It's a shame.

INSPECTOR. (*Crossing to her.*) There are a lot of young women living that sort of existence, Miss Birling, in every city and big town in this country. If there weren't, the factories and warehouses wouldn't know where to look for cheap labor. Ask your father. (BIRLING *sits by fireplace.*)

SHEILA. But these girls aren't cheap labor. They're *people.*

INSPECTOR. (*Drily.*) I've had that notion myself from time to time. In fact, I've thought that it would do us all a bit of good if sometimes we tried to put ourselves in the place of these young women counting their pennies in their dingy little back bedrooms.

SHEILA. Yes, I expect it would. But what happened to her then?

INSPECTOR. She had what seemed to her a wonderful stroke of luck. She was taken on in a shop—and a good shop too—Milward's.

SHEILA. Milward's! We go there—in fact, I was there this afternoon. (*Archly to* GERALD.)—for *your* benefit.

GERALD. (*Smiling.*) Good!

SHEILA. Yes, she was lucky to get taken on at Milward's.

INSPECTOR. That's what she thought. (*Moves few steps toward* SHEILA.) And it happened that at the beginning of December that year—1910—there was a good deal of influenza about, and Milward's suddenly found themselves short-handed. So that gave her her chance. And from what I can gather, she liked working there. It was a nice change from a factory. She enjoyed being among pretty clothes, I've no doubt. And now she felt she was making a good fresh start. You can imagine how she felt.

SHEILA. Yes, of course.

BIRLING. And then she got herself into trouble there, I suppose?

INSPECTOR. (*A step to* BIRLING.) After about a couple of months, just when she felt she was settling down nicely, they told her she'd have to go.

BIRLING. Not doing her work properly?

INSPECTOR. There was nothing wrong with the way she was doing her work. They admitted that.

BIRLING. There must have been something wrong?

INSPECTOR. (*Looks at* SHEILA.) All she knew was—that a customer complained about her—and so she had to go.

SHEILA. (*Staring at him, agitated.*) When was this?

INSPECTOR. (*Impressively, as* BIRLING *crosses* U. R.) At the end of January—last year.

SHEILA. What did this girl look like? (*Rises, crosses* D. R. *to* IN-SPECTOR.)

INSPECTOR. (*Crossing to* D. R.) If you'll come over here, I'll show you. (*He moves down* R. *to floor-lamp—*SHEILA *crosses to him. He produces photograph. She looks at it closely, recognizes it with a little cry, gives half-stifled sob, and then runs out.* INSPECTOR *puts photograph back into his pocket and stares speculatively after her. The other three stare in amazement for a moment and rise.*)

BIRLING. What's the matter with her? (*Crosses* R. C. *Angrily.*) Why the devil do you want to go upsetting the child like that?

INSPECTOR. I didn't do it. She's upsetting herself.

BIRLING. Well—why—why?

INSPECTOR. I don't know—yet. That's something I have to find out.

BIRLING. (*Still angrily.*) Well—if you don't mind—I'll find out first.

GERALD. Shall I go to her?

BIRLING. (*Crossing to door.*) No, leave this to me. I must also have a word with my wife—tell her what's happening. (*Turns at door, staring at* INSPECTOR *angrily.*) We were having a nice family celebration tonight. And a nasty mess you've made of it now, haven't you?

INSPECTOR. (*Steadily, crossing to fireplace.*) That's more or less what I was thinking earlier tonight.

BIRLING. What?

INSPECTOR. When I was in the Infirmary looking at what was left of Eva Smith. A nice little promising life there, I thought, and a nasty mess somebody's made of it. (ERIC *sits.* BIRLING *looks as if about to make some retort, then thinks better of it, and goes out, closing door sharply behind him.* GERALD *and* ERIC *exchange uneasy glances.* INSPECTOR *ignores them.*)

GERALD. (*Crossing to him.*) I'd like to have a look at that photograph now, Inspector.

INSPECTOR. All in good time.

GERALD. I don't see why ——

INSPECTOR. (*Cutting in, massively.*) You heard what I said before, Mr. Croft. One line of inquiry at a time. Otherwise we'll all be talking at once and won't know where we are. If you've anything to tell me, you'll have an opportunity of doing it soon.

GERALD. (*Rather uneasily, crossing up* R.) Well, I don't suppose I have ——

ERIC. (*Suddenly bursting out. Rises.*) Look here, I've had enough of this.

INSPECTOR. (*Drily.*) I daresay.

ERIC. (*Uneasily.*) I'm sorry—but you see—we were having a little party—and I've had a few drinks, including rather a lot of champagne—and I've got a headache—and as I'm only in the way here—I think I'd better turn in. (*Starts to door.*)

INSPECTOR. And I think you'd better stay here.

ERIC. Why should I? (*By doorway.*)

INSPECTOR. It might be less trouble. If you turn in, you might have to turn out again soon.

GERALD. (*Crossing* D. *to* INSPECTOR.) Getting a bit heavy-handed, aren't you, Inspector? (ERIC *crosses* D. *to chair* R. *of table.*)

INSPECTOR. Possibly. But if you're easy with me, I'm easy with you.

GERALD. After all, y'know, we're respectable citizens and not dangerous criminals.

INSPECTOR. Sometimes there isn't as much difference as you think. Often, if it was left to me, I wouldn't know where to draw the line.

GERALD. Fortunately, it isn't left to you, is it?

INSPECTOR. No, it isn't. But some things are left to me. Inquiries of this sort, for instance. (*Enter* SHEILA, *who looks as if she's been crying.*) Well, Miss Birling?

SHEILA. (*Coming in, closing door, crossing to* D. C. *past table.*) You knew it was me all the time, didn't you?

INSPECTOR. I had an idea it might be—(GERALD *crosses to* SHEILA.) from something the girl herself wrote.

SHEILA. I've told my father—he didn't seem to think it amounted to much—but I felt rotten about it at the time, and now I feel a lot worse. (*Crosses to* INSPECTOR.) Did it make much difference to her?

INSPECTOR. Yes, I'm afraid it did. It was the last real steady job she had. When she lost it—for no reason that she could discover—she decided she might as well try another kind of life.

SHEILA. (*Miserably.*) So I'm really responsible? (GERALD *crosses to* U. R. *chair.*)

INSPECTOR. No, not entirely. A good deal happened to her after that. But you're partly to blame. Just as your father is.

ERIC. But what did Sheila do?

SHEILA. (*Distressed, crossing to* R. *of table as* GERALD *sits.*) I went to the manager at Milward's and I told him that if they didn't get rid of that girl, I'd never go near the place again and I'd persuade Mother to close our account with them.

INSPECTOR. And why did you do that?

SHEILA. Because I was in a furious temper.

INSPECTOR. And what had the girl done to make you lose your temper?

SHEILA. When I was looking at myself in the mirror I caught sight of her smiling at the salesgirl, and I was furious with her. I'd been in a bad temper anyhow.

INSPECTOR. And was it the girl's fault?

SHEILA. No, not really. It was my own fault. (*Crosses to* R. *chair. Suddenly, to* GERALD.) All right, Gerald, you needn't look at me like that. At least, I'm trying to tell the truth. I expect you've done things you're ashamed of.

GERALD. (*Surprised.*) Well, I never said I hadn't. I don't see why ——

INSPECTOR. (*Cutting in.*) Never mind about that. You can settle that between you afterwards. (*To* SHEILA.) What happened?

SHEILA. I'd gone in to try something on. It was an idea of my own —— Mother had been against it, and so had the salesgirl—but I insisted. As soon as I tried it on, I knew they'd been right. It just didn't suit me at all. I looked silly in the thing. Well, this girl had brought the dress up from the workroom, and when the salesgirl—Miss Francis—had asked her something about it, this girl, to show us what she meant, had held the dress up, as if she was wearing it. And it just suited her. She was the right type for it, just as I was the wrong type. She was a very pretty girl, too—with soft fine hair and big gray eyes—and that didn't make it any better. Well, when I tried the thing on and looked at myself and knew that it was all wrong, I caught sight of this girl smiling at Miss Francis—as if to say, " Doesn't she look awful? "—and I was absolutely furious. I lost my temper. I was very rude to both of them, and then I went to the manager and told him that this girl had been very impertinent—and—and —— (*She almost breaks down, but just controls herself. Crosses* R. *to chair, sits.* GERALD *rises.* ERIC *crosses* D. L.) How could I know what would happen afterwards? If she'd been some miserable plain little creature, I don't suppose I'd have done it. But she looked as if she could take care of herself. I couldn't be sorry for her.

INSPECTOR. (*Crossing to* SHEILA.) In fact, in a kind of way, you might be said to have been jealous of her?

SHEILA. Yes, I suppose so.

INSPECTOR. And so you used the power you had, as a daughter of a good customer and also of a man well known in the town, to punish the girl just because she made you feel like that.

SHEILA. Yes, but it didn't seem to be anything very terrible at the time. Don't you understand? And if I could help her now, I would ——

INSPECTOR. (*Harshly.*) Yes, but you can't. It's too late. She's dead.

ERIC. My God, it's a bit thick, when you come to think of it ——

SHEILA. (*Stormily. Rises, crosses* D. R. *and to fireplace.*) Oh, shut up, Eric. I know, I know. It's the only time I've ever done anything like that, and I'll never do it again to anybody. I've noticed them giving me a sort of look sometimes at Milward's—I noticed it even this afternoon—and I suppose some of them remember. I feel now I can never go there again. Oh—why had this to happen? (*Goes down* R. *to table.*)

INSPECTOR. (*Sternly, as* GERALD *sits.*) That's what I asked myself tonight when I was looking at that dead girl. And then I said to myself, "Well, we'll try to understand why it had to happen." And that's why I'm here, and why I'm not going until I know all that happened. Eva Smith lost her job with Birling and Company because the strike failed and they were determined not to have another one. At last she found another job—under what name I don't know—in a big shop, and had to leave there because you were annoyed with yourself and passed the annoyance on to her. Now she had to try something else. So first she changed her name to Daisy Renton ——

GERALD. (Startled. Pulling himself together.) Can I get myself a drink, Sheila? (SHEILA merely nods, still staring at him, and he goes across to tantalus on sideboard for a whiskey.)

INSPECTOR. Where is your father, Miss Birling?

SHEILA. He went into the drawing-room. Eric, will you take the Inspector along there, please? (As ERIC moves, INSPECTOR looks from SHEILA to GERALD, then goes out, with ERIC, who opens door. GERALD crosses to just above table, sits in chair.) Well, Gerald?

GERALD. (Trying to smile.) Well what, Sheila?

SHEILA. How did you come to know this girl—Eva Smith?

GERALD. I didn't.

SHEILA. Daisy Renton, then—it's the same thing?

GERALD. Why should I have known her?

SHEILA. (Crossing back of him.) Oh, don't be stupid. We haven't much time. You gave yourself away as soon as he mentioned her other name.

GERALD. All right. I knew her. Let's leave it at that.

SHEILA. We can't leave it at that. (Below armchair.)

GERALD. Now listen, darling —— (Rises, crosses to her.)

SHEILA. No, that's no use. You not only knew her but you knew her very well. Otherwise, you wouldn't look so guilty about it. When did you first get to know her? (He does not reply.) Was it after she left Milward's? When she changed her name, as he said, and began to lead a different sort of life? Were you seeing her last spring and summer, during that time when you hardly came near me and said you were so busy? Were you? (He does not reply, but looks at her.) Yes, of course you were. (Crosses D. R. and sits.)

GERALD. I'm sorry, Sheila. But it was all over and done with, last

26

summer. I haven't set eyes on the girl for at least six months. I don't come into this suicide business.

SHEILA. I thought *J* didn't, half an hour ago.

GERALD. You don't. Neither of us does. (*Crosses to her.*) So—for God's sake—don't say anything to the Inspector!

SHEILA. About you and this girl?

GERALD. Yes. We can keep it from him.

SHEILA. (*Laughs rather hysterically.*) Why—you fool—*he knows!* Of course he knows. And I hate to think how much he knows that we don't know yet. You'll see. You'll see. (*She looks at him almost in triumph. He looks crushed. Door slowly opens and* INSPECTOR *appears, looking steadily and searchingly at them. Door closes, signal for curtain.*)

SLOW CURTAIN

ACT II

SCENE: *The same.*

At rise, scene and situation are exactly as they were at end of Act I, except that main table has been pushed upstage slightly. INSPECTOR *remains at door for a few moments looking at* SHEILA *and* GERALD. *Then comes forward, leaving door open behind him.*
GERALD *steps* L. INSPECTOR *crosses to* U. L. *chair.*

INSPECTOR. (*To* GERALD.) Well?

SHEILA. (*With hysterical laugh, to* GERALD.) You see? What did I tell you?

INSPECTOR. What did you tell him?

GERALD. (*With an effort, crossing* R. C. *below table.*) Inspector, I think Miss Birling ought to be excused from any more of this questioning. She's told you all she knows. She's had a long exciting and tiring day—we were celebrating our engagement, you know—and now she's obviously had about as much as she can stand. You heard her.

SHEILA. He means that I'm getting hysterical now.

INSPECTOR. And are you?

SHEILA. Probably.

INSPECTOR. Well, I don't want to keep you here. I've no more questions to ask you.

SHEILA. No, but you haven't finished asking questions—have you?

INSPECTOR. No.

SHEILA. (*To* GERALD.) You see? (*To* INSPECTOR.) Then I'm staying.

GERALD. (*Crossing to her.*) Why should you? It's bound to be unpleasant and disturbing.

INSPECTOR. And you think young women ought to be protected against unpleasant things?

GERALD. (*Crossing to* C.) If possible—yes.

INSPECTOR. Well, we know one young woman who wasn't, don't we?

GERALD. (*Crossing* U. *to* R. *chair.*) I suppose I asked for that.

SHEILA. Be careful you don't ask for any more, Gerald.

GERALD. (*Crossing to her.*) I only meant to say to you—why stay when you'll obviously hate it?

SHEILA. It can't be any worse for me than it has been. And it might be better.

GERALD. I see ——

SHEILA. What do you see?

GERALD. You've been through it and now you want to see someone else go through it.

SHEILA. (*Bitterly.*) So that's what you think I'm really like! I'm glad I realized it in time, Gerald.

GERALD. No, no, I didn't mean ——

SHEILA. (*Cutting in.*) Yes, you did. And if you'd really loved me, you couldn't have said that. (*Crosses D. R. to table.* GERALD *follows.*) You listened to that nice story about me. I got that girl sacked from Milward's. And now you've made up your mind I must obviously be a selfish vindictive creature.

GERALD. I neither said that, nor even suggested it.

SHEILA. Then why say I want to see somebody else put through it? That's not what I meant at all.

GERALD. (*Crossing D. R.*) All right then, I'm sorry.

SHEILA. (*Turns to D. R. of table.*) Yes, but you don't believe me. And this is just the wrong time not to believe me.

INSPECTOR. (*Massively, taking charge.*) Allow me, Miss Birling. (*To* GERALD *as he crosses to below armchair.*) I can tell you why Miss Birling wants to stay on, and why she says it might be better for her if she did. A girl died tonight. A pretty lively sort of girl, who never did anybody any harm. But she died in misery and agony—hating life ——

SHEILA. (*Distressed. Sits R. chair.*) Don't, please—I know, I know —and I can't stop thinking about it ——

INSPECTOR. (*Ignoring this.*) Now, Miss Birling has just been made to understand what she did to this girl. She feels responsible. And if she leaves us now, and doesn't hear any more, then she'll feel she's entirely to blame, she'll be alone with her responsibility, the rest of tonight, all tomorrow, all the next night ——

SHEILA. (*Eagerly.*) Yes, that's it. And I know I'm to blame—and I'm desperately sorry—but I can't believe—I won't believe—it's simply my fault that in the end she—she committed suicide. That would be too horrible ——

INSPECTOR. (*Sternly to them both.*) You see, we have to share something. If there's nothing else, we'll have to share our guilt.

SHEILA. (*Staring at him.*) Yes. That's true. (*She goes closer to him, wonderingly.*) I don't understand about you?

INSPECTOR. (*Calmly.*) There's no reason why you should.

SHEILA. (*Rises, goes to him.*) I don't know much about police inspectors—but the ones I have met weren't a bit like you.

MRS. BIRLING. (*Enters, smiling, " social."*) Good evening, Inspector. (*At door—then crosses to* D. L. *of table.*)

INSPECTOR. Good evening, madam. (*Crosses to her* D. L. *below table.*)

MRS. BIRLING. (*Same easy tone.*) I'm Mrs. Birling, y'know. My husband has just explained why you're here, and while we'll be glad to tell you anything you want to know, I don't think we can help you much. (GERALD *to alcove.*)

SHEILA. No, Mother—please! (*Crosses* D. L.)

MRS. BIRLING. (*Affecting great surprise.*) What's the matter, Sheila?

SHEILA. (*Hesitantly.*) I know it sounds silly ——

MRS. BIRLING. What does?

SHEILA. (*Sits* D. R.) You see, I feel you're beginning all wrong. And I'm afraid you'll say something or do something that you'll be sorry for afterwards.

MRS. BIRLING. I don't understand you! (*Crosses to her* D. R.)

SHEILA. We all started like that—so confident, so pleased with ourselves, until he began asking us questions. (MRS. BIRLING *looks from* SHEILA *to* INSPECTOR. INSPECTOR *goes to* U. R. *table, crossing above it.*)

MRS. BIRLING. (*Steps to him.*) You seem to have made a great impression on this child, Inspector.

INSPECTOR. (*Coolly.*) We often do on the young ones. They're more impressionable. (*He and* MRS. BIRLING *look at each other for a moment. Then* MRS. BIRLING *turns to* SHEILA *again.*)

MRS. BIRLING. (*Crossing to* SHEILA.) You're looking tired, dear. I think you ought to go to bed—and forget about this absurd business. You'll feel better in the morning.

SHEILA. Mother, I couldn't possibly go. Nothing could be worse for me. We've settled all that. I'm staying here until I know why that girl killed herself.

MRS. BIRLING. (*Steps* L. *a bit.*) Nothing but morbid curiosity.

SHEILA. No, it isn't.

MRS. BIRLING. (*As* GERALD *goes to* D. L. *chair, sits.* MRS. BIRLING *goes to fireplace.*) Please don't contradict me like that. And in any case, I don't suppose for a moment that we can understand why the girl committed suicide. Girls of that class ——

SHEILA. (*Urgently, cutting in.*) Mother, don't—please don't. For your own sake, as well as ours, you mustn't ——

MRS. BIRLING. (*Annoyed.*) Mustn't—what? Really, Sheila!

SHEILA. (*Slowly, carefully now. Rises, crosses to her.*) You mustn't try to build up a kind of wall between us and that girl. If you do, then the Inspector will just break it down. And it'll be all the worse when he does.

MRS. BIRLING. I don't understand you. (*To* INSPECTOR, *crossing to chair* R. *of table.*) Do you?

INSPECTOR. Yes. And she's right.

MRS. BIRLING. (*Haughtily. A step toward him.*) I beg your pardon!

INSPECTOR. (*Very plainly.*) I said yes—I do understand her. And she's right.

MRS. BIRLING. That—I consider—is a trifle impertinent, Inspector. (SHEILA *gives a short, hysterical laugh. Crosses a step toward fender.*) Now, what is it, Sheila?

SHEILA. I don't know. Perhaps it's because *impertinent* is such a silly word. But, Mother, do stop before it's too late.

MRS. BIRLING. If you mean that the Inspector will take of-fense ——?

INSPECTOR. (*Cutting in, calmly.*) No, no. I never take offense.

MRS. BIRLING. I'm glad to hear it. Though I must add that it seems to me that *we* have more reason for taking offense.

INSPECTOR. Let's leave *offense* out of it, shall we?

GERALD. I think we'd better, Mrs. Birling.

SHEILA. So do I.

MRS. BIRLING. (*Rebuking them.*) I'm talking to the Inspector now, if you don't mind. (*To* INSPECTOR, *rather grandly. Crosses and sits armchair above fireplace.*) I realize that you may have to con-duct some sort of inquiry, but I must say that so far you seem to be conducting it in a rather peculiar and offensive manner. You know, of course, that my husband was Lord Mayor only two years ago and that he's still a magistrate?

GERALD. (*Cutting in, rather impatiently.*) Mrs. Birling, the In-

31

spector knows all that. And I don't think it's a very good idea to remind him.

SHEILA. (*Cutting in.*) It's crazy. Stop it, please. Mother!

INSPECTOR. They're right, y'know.

MRS. BIRLING. (*Trying to crush him.*) Really!

INSPECTOR. (*Imperturbable.*) Yes. Now what about Mr. Birling?

MRS. BIRLING. He's coming back in a moment. He's just talking to my son, Eric, who seems to be in an excitable silly mood.

INSPECTOR. What's the matter with him?

MRS. BIRLING. Eric? Oh—I'm afraid he may have had rather too much to drink tonight. We were having a little celebration here ——

INSPECTOR. (*Cutting in.*) Isn't he used to drinking?

MRS. BIRLING. No, of course not. He's only a boy.

INSPECTOR. No, he's a young man.

SHEILA. And he drinks far too much.

MRS. BIRLING. (*Very sharply.*) Sheila!

SHEILA. (*Urgently.*) I don't want to get poor Eric into trouble. He's probably in enough trouble already. But we really must stop these silly pretenses. This isn't the time to pretend that Eric isn't used to drink. He's been steadily drinking too much for the last two years.

MRS. BIRLING. (*Staggered. Rises, crosses down R. C.*) It isn't true. You know him, Gerald—and you're a man—you must know it isn't true.

INSPECTOR. (*As GERALD hesitates. Turning to him.*) Well, Mr. Croft?

GERALD. (*Apologetically, to MRS. BIRLING. Crosses to chair L. of table.*) I'm afraid it is, y'know. Actually I've never seen much of him outside this house—but, well, I have gathered that he does drink pretty hard. (INSPECTOR *crosses U. R. of table.*)

MRS. BIRLING. (*Bitterly.*) And this is the time you choose to tell me!

SHEILA. (*Crossing to her.* GERALD *sits L. chair.*) Yes, of course it is. That's what I meant when I talked about building up a wall that's sure to be knocked flat. It makes it all the harder to bear.

MRS. BIRLING. But it's you—and not the Inspector here—who's doing it ——

SHEILA. Yes, but don't you see? He hasn't started on you yet!

MRS. BIRLING. (*After pause, recovering herself.*) If necessary I shall be glad to answer any questions the Inspector wishes to ask me. Though naturally I don't know anything about this girl. (SHEILA *crosses above* U. *chair of fireplace.*)

INSPECTOR. (*Gravely.*) We'll see, Mrs. Birling. (*Enter* BIRLING, *who closes door behind him.*)

BIRLING. (*Rather hot, bothered. Crosses at door.* SHEILA *crosses* U.) I've been trying to persuade Eric to go to bed, but he won't. Now he says you told him to stay up. Did you? (SHEILA *crosses to armchair.*)

INSPECTOR. Yes, I did.

BIRLING. Why?

INSPECTOR. Because I shall want to talk to him, Mr. Birling.

BIRLING. I can't see why you should, but if you must, then I suggest you do it now. Have him in and get it over, then let the lad go.

INSPECTOR. No, I can't do that yet. I'm sorry, but he'll have to wait.

BIRLING. (*Crossing to him.*) Now look here, Inspector ——

INSPECTOR. (*Cutting in, with authority.*) He must wait his turn.

SHEILA. (*To* MRS. BIRLING.) You see? (*Crosses* U. R., *sits or leans.*)

MRS. BIRLING. No, I don't. And please be quiet, Sheila.

BIRLING. (*Angrily. Crosses to fireplace.*) Inspector, I've told you before, I don't like your tone nor the way you're handling this inquiry. And I don't propose to give you much more rope.

INSPECTOR. You needn't give me any rope.

SHEILA. (*Rather wildly, with laugh.*) No, he's giving us rope—so that we'll hang ourselves!

BIRLING. (*To* MRS. BIRLING.) What's the matter with that child? (*Crosses to fireplace.*)

MRS. BIRLING. Over-excited. And she refuses to go. (*With sudden anger, to* INSPECTOR.) Well, come along—what is it you want to know?

INSPECTOR. (*Coolly.*) At the end of January, last year, this girl Eva Smith had to leave Milward's, because Miss Birling compelled them to discharge her, and then she stopped being Eva Smith, looking for a job, and became Daisy Renton, with other ideas. (*Sharply, turning on* GERALD.) Mr. Croft, when did you first get to know her? (*An exclamation of surprise from* BIRLING *and* MRS. BIRLING.)

33

GERALD. Where did you get the idea that I did know her?

SHEILA. (*Sits on arm of chair above* C. R.) It's no use, Gerald. You're wasting time.

INSPECTOR. As soon as I mentioned the name Daisy Renton, it was obvious you'd known her. You gave yourself away at once.

SHEILA. (*Bitterly.*) Of course he did.

INSPECTOR. And anyhow, I knew already. When and where did you first meet her?

GERALD. (*Crossing* D. L.) All right, if you must have it. I met her first some time in March last year, in the bar at the Palace. I mean the Palace Music Hall here in Brumley ——

SHEILA. Well, we didn't think you meant Buckingham Palace.

GERALD. (*To* SHEILA.) Thanks. You're going to be a great help, I can see. (*Crosses to* L. *table.*) You've said your piece, and you're obviously going to hate this, so why on earth don't you leave us to it?

SHEILA. Nothing would induce me. I want to understand what happens when a man says he's so busy at the works that he can hardly ever find time to come and see the girl he's supposed to be in love with. I wouldn't miss it for ——

INSPECTOR. (*With authority.*) Be quiet, please. Yes, Mr. Croft—in the bar at the Palace Variety Theatre . . .?

GERALD. (*Sits* L. *chair.*) I happened to go down there one night, after a rather long dull day, and as the show wasn't very bright, I went down into the bar for a drink. It's a favorite haunt of women of the town ——

MRS. BIRLING. Women of the town?

INSPECTOR. Prostitutes.

MRS. BIRLING. Yes—but here—in Brumley ——

INSPECTOR. One of the worst cities in the country for prostitution.

BIRLING. Quite true. But I see no point in mentioning the subject—especially —— (*Indicating* SHEILA.)

MRS. BIRLING. It would be much better if Sheila didn't listen to this story at all.

SHEILA. But you're forgetting I'm supposed to be engaged to the hero of it! Go on, Gerald. You went down into the bar, which is a favorite haunt of women of the town.

GERALD. I'm glad I amuse you ——

INSPECTOR. (*Sits* U. R., *sharply.*) Come along, Mr. Croft. What happened?

34

GERALD. I didn't intend to stay down there long. I hate those hard-eyed dough-faced women. But then I noticed a girl who looked quite different. (SHEILA *crosses to* R. *chair, sits.*) She was very pretty—soft brown hair and big dark eyes —— (*He breaks off.*) My God! (*Rises, wanders* L. C.)

INSPECTOR. What's the matter?

GERALD. (*Distressed.*) Sorry—I—well, I've suddenly realized—taken it in properly—that she's dead ——

INSPECTOR. (*Harshly.*) Yes, she's dead. Go on!

GERALD. (*Steps to table.*) This girl was charmingly dressed, too—in a simple inexpensive sort of way—and altogether she looked young and fresh and charming—and—what shall I say?—the opposite of hard and tough, and able to look after herself —— She was quite out of place down there. And obviously she wasn't enjoying herself. Old Joe Meggarty, half-drunk and goggle-eyed, had wedged her into a corner with that obscene fat carcass of his ——

MRS. BIRLING. (*Cutting in.*) There's no need to be disgusting. (*Steps* C.) And surely you don't mean Alderman Meggarty?

GERALD. (*Crosses* D. L., *sits.*) Of course I do. He's a notorious womaniser and one of the worst sots and rogues in Brumley ——

MRS. BIRLING. (*Staggered.*) Well, really! Alderman Meggarty! Well, we *are* learning something tonight! (*Crosses back* D. R., *sits.*)

SHEILA. (*Coolly.*) Of course we are. But everybody knows about that horrible old Meggarty. A girl I know had to see him at the Town Hall one afternoon and she only escaped with a torn blouse ——

BIRLING. (*Sharply shocked.*) Sheila!

INSPECTOR. (*To* GERALD.) Go on.

GERALD. This girl saw me looking at her and then gave me a glance, obviously an S.O.S. So I went across and told Joe Meggarty some nonsense—that the manager had a message for him or something—(*Crosses* U. L. *of table.*) got him out of the way—and then told the girl that if she didn't want any more of that sort of thing, she'd better let me take her out of there. She agreed at once.

INSPECTOR. Where did you go?

GERALD. We went to the County Hotel, which I knew would be quiet at that time of night, and we had a drink or two and talked.

INSPECTOR. Did she drink much at that time?

GERALD. No. She only had a port and lemonade—or some such concoction. All she wanted was to talk—a little friendliness—and I gathered that Joe Meggarty's advances had left her rather shaken—as well they might.

INSPECTOR. She talked about herself?

GERALD. Yes. I asked her questions about herself. She told me her name was Daisy Renton, that she'd lost both parents, that she came originally from somewhere outside Brumley. (*Sits in* L. *chair.*) She also told me she'd had a job in one of the works here and had had to leave after a strike. (BIRLING *crosses* U., *then back.*) She said something about the shop, too, but wouldn't say which it was, and she was deliberately vague about what happened. I couldn't get any exact details from her about her past life. She wanted to talk about herself—just because she felt I was interested and friendly—but at the same time she wanted to be Daisy Renton—and not Eva Smith. In fact, I heard that name for the first time tonight. What she did let slip—though she didn't mean to—was that she was desperately hard up and at that moment was actually hungry. I made the people at the County find some food for her.

INSPECTOR. And then you decided to keep her—as your mistress?

MRS. BIRLING. (*Rising.*) What?

SHEILA. Of course, Mother. It was obvious from the start. Go on, Gerald. Don't mind Mother. (*At* L.)

GERALD. (*Steadily.*) I discovered, not that night but two nights later, when we met again—not accidentally this time, of course— (MRS. BIRLING *crosses behind* D. R. *chair.*) that in fact she hadn't a penny, and was going to be turned out of the miserable back room she had. It happened that a friend of mine, Charlie Brunswick, had gone off to Canada for six months and let me have the key of a nice little set of rooms he had—in Morgan Terrace—and had asked me to keep an eye on them for him and use them if I wanted to. (MRS. BIRLING *sits.*) So I insisted on Daisy moving into those rooms of Charlie's, and I made her take some money to keep her going there. (*Carefully, to* INSPECTOR. SHEILA *above* R. *chair.*) I want you to understand that I didn't install her there so that I could make love to her. That came afterwards. I made her go to Morgan Terrace because I was sorry for her, and didn't like the idea of her going back to the Palace bar. I didn't ask for anything in return.

INSPECTOR. I see.

SHEILA. Yes, but why are you saying that to *him*? You ought to be saying it to me.

GERALD. (*Rises.*) I suppose I ought, really. I'm sorry, Sheila. Somehow I ——

SHEILA. (*Cutting in, as he hesitates.*) I know. Somehow he makes you. (*To* MRS. BIRLING.) He does, y'know.

INSPECTOR. But she became your mistress?

GERALD. Yes. I suppose it was inevitable. She was young and pretty and warm-hearted—and intensely grateful. I became at once the most important person in her life—you understand?

INSPECTOR. Yes. She was a woman. She was lonely. (*To* GERALD.) Were you in love with her?

SHEILA. (*Rises, crosses below chair* R. *of table.*) Just what I was going to ask.

BIRLING. (*Angrily. Rises.*) I really must object ——

INSPECTOR. (*Turning on him sharply.*) Why should you do any protesting? It was you who turned the girl out in the first place.

BIRLING. (*Rather taken aback.*) Well, I only did what any employer might have done. And what I was going to say was that I protest against the way in which my daughter, a young unmarried girl, is being dragged into this ——

INSPECTOR. (*Sharply.*) Your daughter isn't living on the moon. She's here in Brumley too.

SHEILA. (*Crossing to fender to* BIRLING, *who sits.*) Yes, and it was I who had the girl turned out of her job at Milward's. *And* I'm supposed to be engaged to Gerald. And I'm not a child, don't forget. I've a right to know. *Were* you in love with her, Gerald? (BIRLING *crosses to* C., *facing fireplace.*)

GERALD. (*Hesitatingly.*) It's hard to say. I didn't feel about her the way she felt about me.

SHEILA. (*With sharp sarcasm. Crosses to back of* R. *chair.*) Of course not. You were the wonderful Fairy Prince. You must have adored it, Gerald.

GERALD. All right—I did. Nearly any man would have done.

SHEILA. That's probably about the best thing you've said tonight. At least it's honest. Did you see her every night?

GERALD. No. I wasn't telling you a complete lie when I said I'd been very busy at the works all that time. We *were* very busy. But of course I did see a good deal of her.

MRS. BIRLING. (*Rising.*) I don't think we want any further details of this disgusting affair ——

SHEILA. (*Cutting in.*) I do. And anyhow, we haven't had any details yet.

GERALD. (*Rising.*) And you're not going to have any. (*To* MRS. BIRLING.) You know, Mrs. Birling, it wasn't disgusting.

MRS. BIRLING. It's disgusting to me.

SHEILA. (*A step* D. R.) Yes, but you didn't come into this, did you, Mother?

GERALD. Is there anything else you'd like to know—that you ought to know? (SHEILA *crosses above* R. *chair.*)

INSPECTOR. Yes. When did this affair end?

GERALD. I can tell you exactly. In the first week of September. (*Crosses* L. *a bit below door.*) I had to go away for several weeks then—on business—and by that time Daisy knew it was coming to an end. So I broke it off definitely before I went.

INSPECTOR. How did she take it?

GERALD. Better than I'd hoped. She was—very gallant—about it.

SHEILA. (*With irony.*) That was nice for you.

GERALD. No, it wasn't. (*He waits for a moment, then in a low troubled tone.*) She told me she'd been happier than she'd ever been before—but that she knew it couldn't last—hadn't expected it to last. She didn't blame me at all. I wish to God she had now. (*Steps* D. L.) Perhaps I'd feel better about it.

INSPECTOR. She had to leave those rooms?

GERALD. Yes, we'd agreed about that. She'd saved a little money during the summer—she'd lived very economically on what I'd allowed her—and didn't want to take any more from me, but I insisted on a parting gift of enough money—though it wasn't so very much—to see her through to the end of the year.

INSPECTOR. Did she tell you what she proposed to do after you'd left her?

GERALD. No. She refused to talk about that. I got the idea, once or twice from what she said, that she thought of leaving Brumley. Whether she did or not—I don't know. Did she?

INSPECTOR. Yes. She went away for about two months. To some seaside place.

GERALD. By herself?

INSPECTOR. Yes. I think she went away—to be alone, to remember all that had happened between you.

GERALD. (*Steps toward* INSPECTOR.) How do you know that?

INSPECTOR. She kept a rough sort of diary. And she said there that she had to go away and be quiet and remember "just to make it last longer." She felt that there'd never be anything as good for her again—so she had to make it last longer.

GERALD. (*Gravely*.) I see. Well, I never saw her again, and that's all I can tell you.

INSPECTOR. (*Rising*.) It's all I want to know from you.

GERALD. (*Crossing to him*.) In that case—as I'm rather more—upset—by this business than I probably appear to be—and—well, I'd like to be alone for a little while—I'd be glad if you'd let me go.

INSPECTOR. Go? Where? Home?

GERALD. No. I'll just walk out—somewhere by myself. I'll come back.

INSPECTOR. All right, Mr. Croft. (*Crosses to alcove.* GERALD *starts to go.*)

SHEILA. (*Crossing* D. C.) But just in case you forget—or decide not to come back, Gerald, (*Crosses to him* D. L.) I think you'd better take this with you. (*Hands him ring.* BIRLING *rises—takes step to* MRS. BIRLING D. R.)

GERALD. I see. Well, I was expecting this.

SHEILA. I don't dislike you as I did half an hour ago, Gerald. In fact, in some odd way, I rather respect you more than I've ever done before. I knew anyhow you were lying about those months last year when you hardly came near me. I knew there was something fishy about that time. And now at least you've been honest. And I believe what you told us about the way you helped her at first. Just out of pity. And it was my fault really that she was so desperate when you first met her. But this has made a difference. You and I aren't the same people who sat down to dinner here. We'd have to start all over again, getting to know each other ——

BIRLING. (*Steps toward her*.) Now, Sheila, I'm not defending him. But you must understand that a lot of young men ——

SHEILA. Don't interfere, please, Father. Gerald knows what I mean, and you apparently don't.

GERALD. Yes, I know what you mean. (GERALD *goes to door.*

BIRLING *crosses to armchair* D. L., *sits.*) But I'm coming back—if I may.

SHEILA. All right.

MRS. BIRLING. Well, really, I don't know. I think we've just about come to an end of this wretched business ——

GERALD. (*To fireplace on line.*) I don't think so. Excuse me. (*Pause. He goes out.*)

MRS. BIRLING. Well, really—I don't know. (*They watch him go in silence. We hear front door slam.* BIRLING *crosses to* D. R. *chair —stands behind it.* INSPECTOR *at* U. R. *chair.*)

SHEILA. (*To* INSPECTOR, *crossing to doorway.*) You know, you never showed him that photograph of her.

INSPECTOR. No. It wasn't necessary. And I thought it better not to.

MRS. BIRLING. You have a photograph of this girl?

INSPECTOR. (*Crossing between* R. *chair and table.*) Yes. I think you'd better look at it.

MRS. BIRLING. I don't see any particular reason why I should ——

INSPECTOR. Probably not. But you'd better look at it.

MRS. BIRLING. Very well. (*Crosses to him. He produces photograph and she looks hard at it.*)

INSPECTOR. (*Taking back photograph.*) You recognize her?

MRS. BIRLING. No. Why should I?

INSPECTOR. Of course she might have changed lately, but I can't believe she could have changed so much.

MRS. BIRLING. I don't understand you, Inspector?

INSPECTOR. You mean you don't choose to, Mrs. Birling.

MRS. BIRLING. (*Angrily.*) I meant what I said.

INSPECTOR. You're not telling me the truth.

MRS. BIRLING. I beg your pardon!

BIRLING. (*Angrily, to* INSPECTOR. *Crosses to him at fireplace.*) Look here, I'm not going to have this, Inspector. You'll apologize at once.

INSPECTOR. Apologize for what—doing my duty?

BIRLING. No, for being so offensive about it. I'm a public man ——

INSPECTOR. (*Massivly.*) Public men, Mr. Birling, have their responsibilities as well as their privileges.

BIRLING. Possibly. But you weren't asked to come here to talk to me about my responsibilities.

SHEILA. Let's hope not. Though I'm beginning to wonder. (*A step* D. L.)

MRS. BIRLING. Does that mean anything, Sheila? (*Crosses to* SHEILA D. R.)

SHEILA. It means that we've no excuse now for putting on airs and that if we've any sense we won't try. (*Crosses R. C.*) Now you're pretending you don't recognize her from that photograph. (INSPECTOR *crosses to fireplace.*) I admit I don't know why you should, but I know jolly well you did in fact recognize her, from the way you looked. And if you're not telling the truth, why should the Inspector apologize? And can't you see, both of you, you're making it worse? (*She turns away. We hear front door slam again.*)

MRS. BIRLING. (*Sits L. chair.*) Gerald must have come back.

INSPECTOR. Unless your son has just gone out.

BIRLING. I'll see. (*He goes out quickly.* INSPECTOR *turns to* MRS. BIRLING, *at L. table.* SHEILA *crosses above R. chair.*)

INSPECTOR. (*Crossing to fireplace.*) Mrs. Birling, you're a member—a prominent member—of the Brumley Women's Charity Organization, aren't you? (MRS. BIRLING *does not reply.*)

SHEILA. (*Pause.*) Go on, Mother. You might as well admit it. (*To* INSPECTOR.) Yes, she is. Why?

INSPECTOR. (*Calmly.*) It's an organization to which women in distress can appeal for help in various forms. Isn't that so?

MRS. BIRLING. (*With dignity.*) Yes. We've done a great deal of useful work in helping deserving cases.

INSPECTOR. There was a meeting of the interviewing committee two weeks ago?

MRS. BIRLING. I daresay there was.

INSPECTOR. You know very well there was, Mrs. Birling. You were in the chair.

MRS. BIRLING. And if I was, what business is it of yours?

INSPECTOR. (*Severely. Crosses D. L.*) Do you want me to tell you—in plain words? (*Enter* BIRLING, *looking rather agitated.* SHEILA *crosses to alcove.*)

BIRLING. That must have been Eric.

MRS. BIRLING. (*Alarmed.*) Have you been up to his room?

BIRLING. Yes. And I called out on both landings. It must have been Eric we heard go out then.

MRS. BIRLING. Silly boy! Where can he have gone to?

BIRLING. I can't imagine. But he was in one of his excitable queer moods, and even though we don't need him here ——

INSPECTOR. (*Cutting in sharply.*) We do need him here. And if he's not back soon, I shall have to go and find him. (*Crosses to fireplace.* BIRLING *and* MRS. BIRLING *exchange bewildered and rather frightened glances.*)

SHEILA. He's probably just gone to cool off. He'll be back soon.

INSPECTOR. I hope so.

MRS. BIRLING. And why should you hope so?

INSPECTOR. I'll explain why when you've answered my questions, Mrs. Birling.

BIRLING. (*Crossing* D. C. *to* R. *table.*) Is there any reason why my wife should answer questions from you, Inspector?

INSPECTOR. Yes, a very good reason. You'll remember that Mr. Croft told us—quite truthfully, I believe—that he hadn't spoken to or seen Eva Smith since last September. But Mrs. Birling spoke to and saw her only two weeks ago.

SHEILA. (*Astonished, a step to her.*) Mother!

BIRLING. Is this true?

MRS. BIRLING. (*After pause.*) Yes, quite true.

INSPECTOR. She appealed to your organization for help?

MRS. BIRLING. Yes.

INSPECTOR. Not as Eva Smith?

MRS. BIRLING. No. Nor as Daisy Renton.

INSPECTOR. First, she called herself Mrs. Birling ——

BIRLING. (*Astounded.*) *Mrs. Birling!*

MRS. BIRLING. Yes. I think it was simply a piece of gross impertinence—quite deliberate—and naturally that was one of the things that prejudiced me against her case.

BIRLING. (*Crossing* D. R., *sits.*) And I should think so! Damned impudence!

INSPECTOR. You admit being prejudiced against her case?

MRS. BIRLING. Yes.

SHEILA. (*Crossing to* U. L. *table.*) Mother, she's just died a horrible death,—don't forget.

MRS. BIRLING. I'm very sorry. But I think she had only herself to blame.

INSPECTOR. Was it owing to your influence, as the most prominent member of the Committee, that help was refused the girl?

MRS. BIRLING. Possibly.

INSPECTOR. Was it or was it not your influence?

MRS. BIRLING. (*Stung.*) Yes, it was. I didn't like her manner. She'd impertinently made use of our name, though she pretended afterwards it just happened to be the first she thought of. (SHEILA *crosses* D. L., *sits.*) She had to admit, after I began questioning her, that she had no claim to the name, that she wasn't married, and that the story she told at first—about a husband who'd deserted her—was quite false. It didn't take me long to get the truth—or some of the truth—out of her.

INSPECTOR. Why did she want help?

MRS. BIRLING. You know very well why she wanted help.

INSPECTOR. No, I don't. I know why she *needed* help. But as I wasn't there, I don't know what she asked from your committee.

MRS. BIRLING. I don't think we need discuss it.

INSPECTOR. You have no hope of *not* discussing it, Mrs. Birling.

MRS. BIRLING. If you think you can bring any pressure to bear on me, Inspector, you're quite mistaken. (*Rises, crosses to fireplace.*) Unlike the other three, I did nothing I'm ashamed of or that won't bear investigation. The girl asked for assistance. We are asked to look carefully into the claims made upon us. I wasn't satisfied with this girl's claim—she seemed to me to be not a good case—and so I used my influence to have it refused. And in spite of what's happened to the girl since, I consider I did my duty. So if I prefer not to discuss it any further, you have no power to make me change my mind. I've done nothing wrong—and you know it.

INSPECTOR. (*Very deliberately.*) I think you did something terribly wrong—and that you're going to spend the rest of your life regretting it. I wish you'd been with me tonight at the Infirmary. You'd have seen ——

SHEILA. (*Bursting in.*) No, no, please. Not that again. I've imagined it enough already.

INSPECTOR. (*Very deliberately.*) Then the next time you imagine it, just remember that this girl was going to have a child.

SHEILA. (*Horrified. Crosses to* L. *chair, sits.*) No! Oh—horrible—horrible! How could she have wanted to kill herself?

INSPECTOR. Because she'd been turned out and turned down too many times. This was the end.

SHEILA. (*Sits in* L. *chair.*) Mother, you must have known.

INSPECTOR. It was because she was going to have a child that she went for assistance to your mother's committee.

BIRLING. (*Rises.*) Look here, this wasn't Gerald Croft ——

43

INSPECTOR. (*Cutting in, sharply.*) No, no. Nothing to do with him. (BIRLING *sits.*)

SHEILA. Thank goodness for that, anyhow!

INSPECTOR. (*To* MRS. BIRLING.) And you've nothing further to tell me, eh?

MRS. BIRLING. (*Taking step* D. R. *of* INSPECTOR, *going to* R. *chair at table.*) I'll tell you what I told her. Go and look for the father of the child. It's his responsibility.

INSPECTOR. That doesn't make it any the less yours. She came to you for help, at a time when no woman could have needed it more. And you not only refused it yourself, but saw to it that the others refused it, too. She was here alone, friendless, almost penniless, desperate. She needed not only money, but advice, sympathy, friendliness. You've had children. You must have known what she was feeling. And you slammed the door in her face.

SHEILA. (*Rises. With feeling.*) Mother, I think it was cruel and vile.

BIRLING. (*Crossing* D. R. *Dubiously.*) I must say, Sybil, that when this comes out at the inquest, it isn't going to do us much good. The press might easily take it up ——

MRS. BIRLING. (*Crossing* D. R. *Agitated now.*) Oh, stop it, both of you. (*Crosses to* BIRLING.) And please remember before you start accusing me of anything again that it wasn't I who had her turned out of her employment—which probably began it all. (*Turning to* INSPECTOR, *crossing* C. *to him.*) In the circumstances, I think I was justified. The girl had begun by telling us a pack of lies. Afterwards, when I got at the truth, I discovered that she knew who the father was, she was quite certain about that, and so I told her it was her business to make him responsible. (*Crosses to armchair.*) If he refused to marry her—and in my opinion he ought to be compelled to—then he must at least support her.

INSPECTOR. And what did she reply to that?

MRS. BIRLING. (R. *of table.*) Oh—a lot of silly nonsense.

INSPECTOR. What was it?

MRS. BIRLING. (*Sits in chair* R. *of table.*) Whatever it was, I know it made me finally lose all patience with her. She was giving herself ridiculous airs. She was claiming elaborate fine feelings and scruples that were simply absurd in a girl in her position.

INSPECTOR. (*Very sternly.*) Her position now is that she lies with a burnt-out inside on a slab.

44

BIRLING. (*Tries to protest.*) Now look here. (INSPECTOR *turns on him.*)

INSPECTOR. Don't stammer and yammer at me again, man. (BIRLING *sits.*) *What did she say?*

MRS. BIRLING. (*Rather cowed.*) She said that the father was only a youngster—silly, wild, and drinking too much. There couldn't be any question of marrying him—it would be wrong for them both. He had given her money, but she didn't want to take any more money from him.

INSPECTOR. Why didn't she want to take any more money from him?

MRS. BIRLING. All a lot of nonsense—I didn't believe a word of it.

INSPECTOR. I'm not asking you if you believed it. I want to know what she said. Why didn't she want to take any more money from this boy?

MRS. BIRLING. Oh—she had some fancy reason. As if a girl of that sort would ever refuse money!

INSPECTOR. (*Sternly. Crosses in a bit.*) I warn you, you're making it worse for yourself. What reason did she give for not taking any more money?

MRS. BIRLING. Her story was—that he'd said something one night, when he was drunk, that gave her the idea that it wasn't his money.

INSPECTOR. Where had he got it from then?

MRS. BIRLING. He'd stolen it.

INSPECTOR. So she'd come to you for assistance because she didn't want to take stolen money?

MRS. BIRLING. That's the story she finally told, after I'd refused to believe her original story—that she was a married woman who'd been deserted by her husband. I didn't see any reason to believe that one story should be any truer than the other. Therefore you're quite wrong to suppose I shall regret what I did.

INSPECTOR. But if her story was true, if this boy had been giving her stolen money, then she came to you for help because she wanted to keep this youngster out of any more trouble—isn't that so?

MRS. BIRLING. Possibly. But it sounded ridiculous to me. So I was perfectly justified in advising my Committee not to allow her claim for assistance.

INSPECTOR. You're not even sorry now, when you know what happened to the girl?

MRS. BIRLING. I'm sorry she should have come to such a horrible end. But I accept no blame for it at all.

INSPECTOR. Who is to blame then?

MRS. BIRLING. First, the girl herself. (SHEILA *steps* R. *below door.*) Secondly, I blame the young man who was the father of the child she was going to have. If, as she said, he didn't belong to her class, and was some drunken young idler, then that's all the more reason why he shouldn't escape.

INSPECTOR. And if her story is true—that he was stealing money——?

MRS. BIRLING. (*Rather agitated now. Rises, crosses* D. L. *to* D. L. *corner of table. Pacing.*) There's no point in assuming that . . .

INSPECTOR. But suppose we do, what then?

MRS. BIRLING. Then he'd be entirely responsible ——

INSPECTOR. So he's the chief culprit anyhow.

MRS. BIRLING. Certainly. And he ought to be dealt with very severely ——

SHEILA. (*With sudden alarm.*) Mother—stop—stop! (*Crosses* D. L. *of her above table.*)

BIRLING. Be quiet, Sheila!

SHEILA. But don't you see —— (*A step* R.)

MRS. BIRLING. (*Severely.*) You're behaving like a hysterical child tonight! (SHEILA, *at* U. R. *table, begins crying quietly.* MRS. BIRLING *turns to* INSPECTOR. *Crosses down* R. *to table.*) And if you'd take some steps to find this young man and then make sure that he's compelled to confess in public his responsibility—instead of staying here asking quite unnecessary questions—then you really would be doing your duty.

INSPECTOR. (*Grimly.*) Don't worry, Mrs. Birling. I shall do my duty. (*Looks at his watch.*)

MRS. BIRLING. (*Triumphantly.*) I'm glad to hear it. (*Turns away from him.*) And now, no doubt, you'd like to say good night. (*Crosses to doorway.*)

INSPECTOR. Not yet. I'm waiting.

MRS. BIRLING. Waiting for what?

INSPECTOR. To do my duty. (BIRLING *rises.*)

SHEILA. (*Distressed.*) Now, Mother—don't you see? (*Crosses* D. R. C.)

MRS. BIRLING. (*Two steps to* SHEILA, *to* INSPECTOR, *then door slams. Understanding now.*) But surely . . . I mean . . . It's ridiculous . . . (*At* D. C. *chair, crosses to* L. *chair, ready to collapse. She stops and exchanges a frightened glance with* BIRLING.)

BIRLING. (*Terrified now, rises, goes to* C.) Look, Inspector, you're not trying to tell us that—that my boy—is mixed up in this ——?

INSPECTOR. (*Sternly.*) If he is, then we know what to do, don't we? Mrs. Birling has just told us.

BIRLING. (*Thunderstruck.*) My God! But—look here —— (*Crosses and sits* D. R.)

MRS. BIRLING. (*Agitated. Sits* L. *chair above.*) I don't believe it. I won't believe it. . . .

SHEILA. (*Crossing to her.*) Mother—I begged you and begged you to stop —— (INSPECTOR *holds up a hand. We hear front door. They wait, looking toward door.* ERIC *enters, looking extremely pale and distressed. He meets their inquiring stares.*)

CURTAIN FALLS SLOWLY

ACT III

SCENE: *The same.*

Exactly as at end of Act II. ERIC *is standing just inside the room and the others are staring at him.*

ERIC. (*Crossing to* INSPECTOR.) You know, don't you? (BIRLING *sits down* R.)

INSPECTOR. (*As before.*) Yes, we know. (ERIC *shuts door and comes further in.*)

MRS. BIRLING. (*Distressed, on* L. *chair.*) Eric, I can't believe it. There must be some mistake. You don't know what we've been saying.

SHEILA. (U. R. *of* MRS. BIRLING.) It's a good job for him he doesn't, isn't it?

ERIC. Why?

SHEILA. Because Mother's been busy blaming everything on the young man who got this girl into trouble, and saying he shouldn't escape and should be made an example of ——

BIRLING. (*Below fireplace.*) That's enough, Sheila.

ERIC. (*Bitterly.*) You haven't made it any easier for me, have you, Mother?

MRS. BIRLING. But I didn't know it was *you*—I never dreamt. Besides, you're not that type—you don't get drunk ——

SHEILA. (*Crossing below* MRS. BIRLING.) Of course he does. I told you he did.

ERIC. (*Steps to her.*) *You* told her. Why, you little sneak!

SHEILA. No, that's not fair, Eric. I could have told her months ago, but of course I didn't. I only told her tonight because I knew everything was coming out—it was simply bound to come out to-night—so I thought she might as well know in advance.—I've already been through it, don't forget.

MRS. BIRLING. Sheila, I simply don't understand your attitude.

BIRLING. Neither do I. If you'd had any sense of loyalty ——

INSPECTOR. (*Cutting in smoothly. A step downstage.*) Just a minute, Mr. Birling. There'll be plenty of time, when I've gone, for you all to adjust your family relationships. But now I must hear what your son has to tell me. (*Sternly, to the three of them.*) And I'll be obliged if you'll let us get on without any further interruptions. (*Turning to* ERIC.)

ERIC. (*Miserably.*) Could I have a drink first?

BIRLING. (*Explosively.*) No.

INSPECTOR. (*Firmly.*) Yes. (*As* BIRLING *looks like interrupting explosively.*) I know—he's your son and this is your house—but look at him.

BIRLING. (*To* ERIC.) All right. Go on. (ERIC *goes for a whiskey. His whole manner of handling the decanter and then the drink shows his familiarity with quick heavy drinking. The others watch him narrowly.* BIRLING *crosses down* R. *Bitterly.*) I understand a lot of things now that I didn't understand before. (*Crosses* L. *of* MRS. BIRLING.)

INSPECTOR. Don't start on that. I want to get on. (*To* ERIC.) When did you first meet this girl?

ERIC. (*At* R. *chair.*) One night last November.

INSPECTOR. Where did you meet her?

ERIC. In the Palace bar. I'd been there an hour or so with two or three chaps. I was a bit squiffy.

INSPECTOR. What happened then?

ERIC. I began talking to her, and stood her a few drinks. I was rather far gone by the time we had to go.

INSPECTOR. Was she drunk, too?

ERIC. She told me afterwards that she was a bit, chiefly because she'd not had much to eat that day.

INSPECTOR. Had she gone there—to solicit?

ERIC. No, she hadn't. She wasn't that sort, really. But—well, I suppose she didn't know what to do. There was some woman who wanted her to go there. I never quite understood about that.

INSPECTOR. You went with her to her lodgings that night?

ERIC. Yes, I insisted—it seems. I'm not very clear about it, but afterwards she told me she didn't want me to go in, but that—well, I was in that state when one easily turns nasty—and I threatened to make a row.

INSPECTOR. So she let you in?

ERIC. Yes. And that's when it happened. And I didn't even remember—that's the hellish part. Oh—my God! How stupid it all is! (*Crosses to* D. C. *chair—sits.*)

MRS. BIRLING. (*Rises. With a cry.*) Oh—Eric—how could you?

BIRLING. (*Sharply.*) Sheila, take your mother along to the drawing-room ——

SHEILA. (*Protesting.*) But—I want to ——

BIRLING. (*Very sharply.*) You heard what I said. (*Gentler.*) Go on, Sybil. (SHEILA *takes* MRS. BIRLING *out. Then* BIRLING *closes door and comes in.* ERIC *sits* C., INSPECTOR *at fireplace.*)

INSPECTOR. (*Crossing down to* ERIC.) When did you see her again?

ERIC. About a fortnight afterwards.

INSPECTOR. By appointment?

ERIC. No. And I couldn't remember her name or where she lived. It was all very vague. But I happened to see her again in the Palace bar.

INSPECTOR. More drinks?

ERIC. Yes, though this time I wasn't so bad.

INSPECTOR. But you went to her room again?

ERIC. Yes. And this time we talked a bit. She told me something about herself and I talked, too. Told her my name and what I did.

INSPECTOR. And you made love again?

ERIC. Yes. (INSPECTOR *crosses* U. *to* U. L. *corner of table.*) I wasn't in love with her or anything—but I liked her—she was pretty and a good sport ——

BIRLING. (*Harshly. Crosses to him.*) So you had to go to bed with her?

ERIC. (*Rises.*) Well, I'm old enough to be married, aren't I? And I'm not married, and I hate these fat old tarts round the town—the ones I see some of your respectable friends with ——

BIRLING. (*Angrily.*) I don't want any of that talk from you —— (*Crosses to* ERIC.)

INSPECTOR. (*Very sharply.* BIRLING *crosses down* R.) I don't want any of it from either of you. Settle it afterwards. (*Crosses down to down* L. *of table.*) Did you arrange to see each other after that?

ERIC. Yes. And the next time—or the time after that—she told me she thought she was going to have a baby. She wasn't quite sure. And then she was.

INSPECTOR. Of course. And of course she was worried?

ERIC. (*Sits in chair below table.*) Yes, and so was I. I was in a hell of a state about it.

INSPECTOR. Did she suggest that you ought to marry her?

ERIC. No. She didn't want me to marry her. Said I didn't love her—and all that. In a way, she treated me—as if I were a kid. Though I was nearly as old as she was.

INSPECTOR. So what did you propose to do?

ERIC. Well, she hadn't a job—and didn't feel like trying again for one—and she'd no money left—so I insisted on giving her enough money to keep her going—until she refused to take any more ——

INSPECTOR. How much did you give her altogether?

ERIC. I suppose—about fifty pounds all told.

BIRLING. (*Steps up to fireplace.*) Fifty pounds—on top of drinking and going round the town! Where did you get fifty pounds from? (ERIC *does not reply.*)

INSPECTOR. (*Crossing to* L. *chair.*) That's my question, too.

ERIC. (*Miserably. Rises, crosses to* R. *of table.*) I got it—from the office ——

BIRLING. *My* office?

ERIC. Yes.

INSPECTOR. You mean—you stole the money?

ERIC. Not really.

BIRLING. (*Angrily.*) What do you mean—*not really?* (ERIC *does not reply because now* MRS. BIRLING *and* SHEILA *come back.* ERIC *sits* R. *of table.*)

SHEILA. This isn't my fault. (*Sits down* L.)

MRS. BIRLING. (*To* BIRLING, *crossing to him.*) I'm sorry, Arthur, but I simply couldn't stay in there. I had to know what's happening.

BIRLING. (*Savagely.*) Well, I can tell you what's happening! He's admitted he was responsible for the girl's condition, and now he's telling us he supplied her with money he stole from the office.

MRS. BIRLING. (*Shocked. Crosses to fireplace.*) Eric! You stole money?

ERIC. No, not really. I intended to pay it back.

BIRLING. We've heard that story before. How could you have paid it back?

ERIC. I'd have managed somehow. I had to have some money ——

BIRLING. I don't understand how you could take as much as that out of the office without somebody knowing.

ERIC. There were some small accounts to collect, and I asked for cash ——

BIRLING. Gave the firm's receipt and then kept the money, eh?

ERIC. Yes.

BIRLING. (*Crossing up and down.*) You must give me a list of those accounts. I've got to cover this up as soon as I can. You damned fool—why didn't you come to me when you found yourself in this mess? (INSPECTOR *goes* U. L. *to table.*)

ERIC. Because you're not the kind of father a chap could go to when he's in trouble—that's why. (MRS. BIRLING *crosses down* R., *sits in chair* R.)

BIRLING. (*Angrily.*) Don't talk to me like that. Your trouble is—you've been spoilt.

INSPECTOR. (*Cutting in.* BIRLING *crosses to* L. *alcove.*) And my trouble is—that I haven't much time. You'll be able to divide the responsibility between you when I'm gone. (*To* ERIC.) Just one last question, that's all. The girl discovered that this money you were giving her was stolen, didn't she?

ERIC. (*Miserably.*) Yes. That was the worst of all. She wouldn't take any more, and she didn't want to see me again. (*Sudden startled tone. Rises, crosses below table to* INSPECTOR *at* D. L *table.*) Here, but how did you know that? Did she tell you?

INSPECTOR. No. She told me nothing. I never spoke to her.

SHEILA. She told Mother.

MRS. BIRLING. (*Alarmed.*) Sheila!

SHEILA. Well, Eric has to know.

ERIC. (*To* MRS. BIRLING.) She told you? Did she come here—but then she couldn't have done that, she didn't even know I lived here. What happened? (MRS. BIRLING, *distressed, shakes her head, but does not reply.*) Come on, don't just look like that. Tell me—tell me—what happened?

INSPECTOR. (*With calm authority. Crosses to* U. L. *table.*) I'll tell you. She went to your mother's committee for help. Your mother refused that help.

ERIC. (*Nearly at breaking point. At* R. *table.*) Then—you killed her! She came to you to protect me—and you turned her away—yes, and you killed her—and the child she'd have had, too—my child—your own grandchild—you killed them both—damn you, damn you ——

MRS. BIRLING. (*Very distressed now. Rises, a step toward fireplace.*) No—Eric—please—I didn't know—I didn't understand ——

52

ERIC. (*Almost threatening her. Crosses to her.*) You don't under-stand anything—you never did. You never even tried—you ——
SHEILA. (*Rises, frightened.*) Eric, don't—don't ——
BIRLING. (*Furious, intervening, crossing to them.*) Why, you hysterical young fool—get back—or I'll ——
INSPECTOR. (*Taking charge, masterfully.*) Stop! (BIRLING *crosses to fireplace*—ERIC *crosses to* R. *chair, sits. They are suddenly quiet, staring at him.* MRS. BIRLING *crosses down* R., *sits.*) I don't need to know any more. Neither do you. This girl killed herself—and died a horrible death. But each of you helped to kill her. Remember that. Never forget it. (*He looks from one to other, carefully.*) But then I don't think you ever will. Remember what you did, Mrs. Birling. You turned her away when she most needed help. You refused her even the pitiable little bit of organized charity you had in your power to grant her. Remember what you did ——
ERIC. (*Unhappily.*) My God—I'm not likely to forget!
INSPECTOR. Just used her for the end of a stupid drunken eve-ning, as if she was an animal, a thing, not a person. No, you won't forget. (*Looks at* SHEILA.)
SHEILA. (*Bitterly. Crosses below chest.*) I know. I had her turned out of a job. I started it.
INSPECTOR. You helped—but didn't start it. (*Rather savagely, to* BIRLING.) You started it. She wanted twenty-five shillings a week instead of twenty-two. You made her pay a heavy price for that. And now she'll make you pay a heavier price still.
BIRLING. (*Unhappily.*) Look, Inspector—I'd give thousands—yes. thousands —— (ERIC *at* U. L. *table.*)
INSPECTOR. You're offering the money at the wrong time, Mr. Birling. (*He makes move as if concluding the session, possibly shutting up note-book, etc. Then surveys them sardonically.*) No, I don't think any of you will forget. Nor that young man, Croft, though he had some affection for her at least, and made her happy for a time. Well, Eva Smith's gone. You can't do her any more harm. And you can't do her any good now, either. You can't even say, " I'm sorry, Eva Smith."
SHEILA. (*Who is crying quietly.*) That's the worst of it.
INSPECTOR. (*Steps* C.) One Eva Smith has gone—but there are millions and millions of Eva Smiths and John Smiths still left with us, with their lives, their hopes and fears, their suffering and chance

of happiness, all intertwined with our lives, with what we think and say and do. We don't live alone. We are members of one body. We are responsible for each other. And I tell you that the time will soon come when if men will not learn that lesson, then they will be taught it in fire and blood and anguish. We don't live alone. Good night. (*He walks straight out, leaving them staring, subdued and wondering.* SHEILA *is still crying quietly.* MRS. BIRLING *has collapsed into a chair.* ERIC *is brooding desperately.* BIRLING, *the only active one, hears front door slam, moves hesitatingly toward door, stops, looks gloomily at other three, then pours himself a drink, which he hastily swallows.* ERIC *crosses to* U. L. *chair, sits.* BIRLING *crosses up to window, opens it, and crosses to* R. *table.*)

BIRLING. (*Angrily, to* ERIC.) You're the one I blame for this.

ERIC. I'll bet I am.

BIRLING. (*Angrily. Crosses down.*) Yes, and you don't realize yet all you've done. Most of this is bound to come out. There'll be a public scandal.

ERIC. Well, I don't care now.

BIRLING. (*At fireplace.*) You! You don't seem to care about any-thing. But I care. I was almost certain for a knighthood in the next honors' list —— (*Crosses to* L. *chair.* ERIC *laughs rather hysterically, pointing at him.*)

ERIC. (*Laughing.*) Oh—for God's sake! What does it matter now whether they give you a knighthood or not?

BIRLING. (*Stormily.*) It doesn't matter to *you!* Apparently noth-ing matters to you. But it may interest you to know that until every penny of that money you stole is repaid, you'll work for nothing. And there's going to be no more of this drinking round town—picking up women in the Palace bar —— (*Crosses behind table to fireplace.*)

MRS. BIRLING. (*Coming to life.*) I should think not. Eric, I'm absolutely ashamed of you.

ERIC. Well, I don't blame you. But don't forget I'm ashamed of you as well—yes, both of you.

BIRLING. (*Angrily.*) Drop that. There's every excuse for what both your mother and I did—it turned out unfortunately, that's all ——

SHEILA. (*Scornfully.*) That's all.

BIRLING. Well, what have you to say?

SHEILA. I don't know where to begin. (*Crosses to* BIRLING.)

BIRLING. Then don't begin. Nobody wants you to. (*Crosses to fireplace.*)

SHEILA. (*Steps to* BIRLING.) I behaved badly, too. I know I did. I'm ashamed of it. But now you're beginning all over again to pretend that nothing much has happened —

BIRLING. Nothing much has happened! Haven't I already said there'll be a public scandal—unless we're lucky—and I'm the one who'll suffer.

SHEILA. But that's not what I'm talking about. I don't care about that. The point is, you don't seem to have learnt anything.

BIRLING. Don't I? Well, you're quite wrong there. I've learnt plenty tonight. And you don't want me to tell you what I've learnt, I hope? When I look back on tonight—when I think of what I was feeling when the five of us sat down to dinner at that table — (*Sits* R. *chair.*)

ERIC. (*Cutting in.* SHEILA *crosses to* L. *chair.*) Yes, and do you remember what you said to Gerald and me after dinner, when you were feeling so pleased with yourself? You told us that a man has to make his own way, and that we weren't to take any notice of these cranks who tell us that everybody has to look after everybody else, as if we were all mixed up together. Do you remember? Yes—and then one of those cranks walked in—the Inspector. (*Laughs bitterly.*) I didn't notice you told him that it's every man for himself.

SHEILA. (*Sharply attentive. Steps to* ERIC, *crosses back.*) Is that when the Inspector came, just after Father had said that?

ERIC. Yes. What of it? (SHEILA *comes* R. C.)

MRS. BIRLING. (*With some excitement.*) Now what's the matter, Sheila?

SHEILA. It doesn't matter much now, of course—but *was* he really a Police Inspector?

BIRLING. Well, if he wasn't, it matters a devil of a lot. Makes all the difference.

SHEILA. (*Crossing to him.*) No, it doesn't.

BIRLING. Don't talk rubbish. Of course it does.

SHEILA. (*Crossing to* BIRLING.) Well, it doesn't to me. And it oughtn't to you, either.

MRS. BIRLING. Don't be childish, Sheila.

SHEILA. (*Flaring up. Rises.*) I'm not being. If you want to know, it's you two who are being childish—trying not to face the facts.

55

BIRLING. I won't have that sort of talk. Any more of that and you leave this room.

ERIC. That'll be terrible for her, won't it?

SHEILA. (*Crossing to* L. *chair, sits.*) I'm going anyhow in a minute or two. But don't you see, if all that's come out tonight is true, then it doesn't much matter who it was who made us confess? And it *was* true, wasn't it? That's what's important—and it's what we did that's important—and not whether a man is a Police Inspector or not.

ERIC. He was our Police Inspector, all right. (*Sits* D. L.)

SHEILA. That's what I mean, Eric. (*Turning to her parents.*) But if it's any comfort to you—and it isn't to me—I have an idea— and I had it all along vaguely—that there was something curious about him. (*To* BIRLING.) He never seemed like an ordinary Police Inspector.

BIRLING. (*Rather excited. Rises.*) You're right. I felt it too. (*Crosses to* MRS. BIRLING. SHEILA *crosses to* U. L. *table.*) Didn't you?

MRS. BIRLING. Well, I must say his manner was quite extraordinary: so—so rude—and assertive ——

BIRLING. Then look at the way he talked to me. Telling me to shut up—and so on. He must have known I was an ex-Lord Mayor and a magistrate and so forth. Besides—the way he talked —you remember. I mean, they don't talk like that. I've had dealings with dozens of them.

SHEILA. All right. But it doesn't make any real difference, y'know.

MRS. BIRLING. Of course it does.

ERIC. No, Sheila's right. It doesn't.

BIRLING. (*Angrily. Crosses* L. *a bit.*) That's comic, that is, coming from you! You're the one it makes *most* difference to. You've confessed to theft, and now he knows all about it, and he can bring it out at the inquest, and then if necessary carry it to court. He can't do anything to your mother and Sheila and me—except perhaps make us look a bit ashamed of ourselves in public—but as for you, he can ruin you. And then you tell us it doesn't make any real difference. It makes *all* the difference. (*Crosses to fireplace.*)

SHEILA. (*Slowly.*) You know, all *he* did really was to make *us* confess. We hardly ever told him anything he didn't know. Did you notice that?

BIRLING. That's nothing. He had a bit of information, left by the girl, and made a few smart guesses—but the fact remains that if you hadn't talked so much, he'd really have had little to go on. (*Looks angrily at them.*) And really, when I come to think of it, why you all had to go letting everything come out like that, beats me.

SHEILA. It's all right talking like that now. But he made us confess.

MRS. BIRLING. He certainly didn't make me confess—as you call it. I told him quite plainly that I thought I had done no more than my duty.

SHEILA. Oh—Mother!

BIRLING. The fact is, you allowed yourselves to be bluffed. Yes—bluffed.

MRS. BIRLING. (*Protesting.*) Now really—Arthur.

BIRLING. No, not you, my dear. But these two. That fellow obviously didn't like us. He was prejudiced from the start. Probably a Socialist or some sort of crank—he talked like one. And then, instead of standing up to him, you let him bluff you into talking about your private affairs. You ought to have stood up to him.

ERIC. (*Sulkily.*) Well, I didn't notice you standing up to him.

BIRLING. No, because by that time you'd admitted you'd been taking money. What chance had I after that? I was a fool not to have insisted upon seeing him alone.

ERIC. That wouldn't have worked.

SHEILA. Of course it wouldn't.

MRS. BIRLING. (*Crossing to R. chair, sits.*) Really, from the way you children talk, you might be wanting to help *him*, instead of us. Now just be quiet so that your father can decide what we ought to do. (*Looks expectantly at* BIRLING.)

BIRLING. (*Dubiously, crossing R. C.*) Yes—well. We'll have to do something—and get to work quickly, too. (*Pause. As he now hesitates there is a ring at front door. They look at each other in alarm.*) Now who's this? Had I better go? (ERIC *rises.*)

MRS. BIRLING. No. Edna'll go. I asked her to wait up to make us some tea.

SHEILA. It might be Gerald coming back? (ERIC *to alcove.* SHEILA *at* U. L. *table.*)

BIRLING. (*Relieved. A step down R.*) Yes, of course. I'd forgotten about him. (EDNA *appears.*)

EDNA. It's Mr. Croft. (GERALD *appears,* EDNA *withdraws.*)

GERALD. I hope you don't mind my coming back? (*Crosses* R. *to* BIRLING.) I had a special reason for doing so. When did that Inspector go?

SHEILA. Only a few minutes ago. He put us all through it ——

MRS. BIRLING. (*Warningly*.) Sheila!

SHEILA. Gerald might as well know.

BIRLING. (*Hastily*.) Now—now—we needn't bother him with all that stuff.

SHEILA. All right. (*To* GERALD.) But we're all in it—up to the neck. It got worse after you left.

GERALD. How did he behave?

SHEILA. He was—frightening.

BIRLING. If you ask me, he behaved in a very peculiar and suspicious manner.

MRS. BIRLING. The rude way he spoke to Mr. Birling and me—it was quite extraordinary! Why? (*They all look inquiringly at* GERALD.)

BIRLING. (*Excitedly*.) You know something. What is it?

GERALD. (*Slowly*.) That man wasn't a police officer.

BIRLING. (*Astounded*.) What?

MRS. BIRLING. Are you certain?

GERALD. I'm almost certain. That's what I came back to tell you.

BIRLING. (*Excitedly*.) Good lad! You asked about him, eh?

GERALD. Yes. I met a police sergeant I know down the road. I asked him about this Inspector Goole and described the chap carefully to him. He swore there wasn't any Inspector Goole or anybody like him on the force here.

BIRLING. You didn't tell him ——?

GERALD. (*Cutting in*.) No, no. I passed it off by saying I'd been having an argument with somebody. But the point is—this sergeant was dead certain they hadn't any inspector at all like the chap who came here.

BIRLING. (*Excitedly*.) By jingo! A fake!

MRS. BIRLING. (*Triumphantly*.) Didn't I tell you? Didn't I say I couldn't imagine a real police inspector talking like that to us?

GERALD. Well, you were right. There isn't any such inspector. We've been had.

BIRLING. (*Beginning to move. Crosses* D. R.) I'm going to make certain of this.

MRS. BIRLING. (GERALD *crosses to alcove.*) What are you going to do?

BIRLING. Ring up the Chief Constable—Colonel Roberts.

MRS. BIRLING. (*Crossing to fireplace.*) Careful what you say, dear.

BIRLING. (*Now at telephone.*) Of course. (SHEILA *crosses in a bit.*) Brumley 5721. (*To others, as he waits.*) I was going to do this anyhow. I've had my suspicions all along. (*Into phone.*) Roberts, please. Mr. Arthur Birling here. . . . Oh, Roberts— Birling. Sorry to ring you up so late, but can you tell me if an Inspector Goole has joined your staff lately . . . ? Goole. G-O-O-L-E . . . a new man. (*Here he may describe the appearance of actor playing* INSPECTOR.) I see . . . yes . . . well, that settles it. . . . No, just a little argument we were having here. . . . Good night. (*Puts down phone and looks at others. Crosses* R. *to chair.*) There's nobody who even looks like the man who came here. That man definitely wasn't a police inspector at all. As Gerald says—we've been had. (GERALD *sits* L. *chair.*)

MRS. BIRLING. I felt it all the time. He never talked like one. He never even looked like one. (*Crosses to* D. R. *chair, sits.*)

BIRLING. This makes a difference, y'know. In fact, it makes all the difference.

SHEILA. (*Bitterly.*) I suppose we're all nice people now!

BIRLING. If you've nothing more sensible than that to say, Sheila, you'd better keep quiet.

ERIC. (*At* U. L. *end of table.*) She's right, though.

BIRLING. (*Angrily.*) And you'd better keep quiet, anyhow! If that *had* been a police inspector and he'd heard you confess ——

MRS. BIRLING. (*Warningly.*) Arthur—careful! (ERIC *crosses to alcove.*)

BIRLING. (*Hastily.*) Yes, yes.

SHEILA. (*Sits* U. R. *chair.*) You see, Gerald, you don't happen to know the rest of our crimes and idiocies.

GERALD. That's all right, I don't want to. (*To* BIRLING.) What do you make of this business now? Was it a hoax? (ERIC *at* U. *window.*)

BIRLING. Of course. Somebody put that fellow up to coming here and hoaxing us. Believe it or not, there are people in this town who dislike me enough to do that. We ought to have seen through it from the first. In the ordinary way, I believe I would have done. But coming like that, bang on top of our little celebration, just when we were all feeling so pleased with ourselves, naturally it took me by surprise.

MRS. BIRLING. (*At* D. R. *chair.*) I wish I'd been here when that man first arrived. I'd have asked *him* a few questions before I allowed him to ask us any.

SHEILA. It's all right saying that now.

MRS. BIRLING. I was the only one of you who didn't give in to him. And now I say we must discuss this business quietly and sensibly and decide if there's anything to be done about it. (ERIC *passes alcove entrance.*)

BIRLING. (*With hearty approval.*) You're absolutely right, my dear. Already we've discovered one important fact—that that fellow was a fraud and we've been hoaxed—and that may not be the end of it by any means.

GERALD. I'm sure it isn't.

BIRLING. (*Keenly interested.*) You are, eh? Good! (*To* ERIC, *who is restless.*) Eric, sit down.

ERIC. (*Sulkily.*) I'm all right.

BIRLING. All right? You're anything but all right. And you needn't stand there—as if—as if ——

ERIC. As if—what?

BIRLING. As if you'd nothing to do with us. Just remember your own position, young man. If anybody's up to the neck in this business, you are, so you'd better take some interest in it.

ERIC. I do take some interest in it. I take too much, that's my trouble.

SHEILA. It's mine, too.

BIRLING. Now listen, you two. If you're still feeling on edge, then the least you can do is to keep quiet. Leave this to us. I'll admit that fellow's antics rattled us a bit. But we've found him out—and all we have to do is to keep our heads. Now it's our turn.

SHEILA. Our turn to do—what?

MRS. BIRLING. (*Sharply.*) To behave sensibly, Sheila—which is more than you're doing.

ERIC. (*Crossing to* BIRLING. *Bursting out.*) What's the use of talking about behaving sensibly? You're beginning to pretend now that nothing's really happened at all. And I can't see it like that. This girl's still dead, isn't she? Nobody's brought her to life, have they?

SHEILA. (*Eagerly.*) That's just what I feel, Eric. And it's what they don't seem to understand.

60

ERIC. Whoever that chap was, the fact remains that I did what I did. And Mother did what she did. And the rest of you did what you did to her. It's still the same rotten story whether it's been told to a police inspector or to somebody else. According to you, I ought to feel a lot better ——— (*To* GERALD.) I stole some money, Gerald, you might as well know ——— (*As* BIRLING *tries to interrupt.*) I don't care, let him know. The money's not the important thing. It's what happened to the girl and what we all did to her that matters. And I still feel the same about it, and that's why I don't feel like sitting down and having a nice cozy talk.

SHEILA. (*Rising.*) And Eric's absolutely right. And it's the best thing any one of us has said tonight and it makes me feel a bit less ashamed of us. You're just beginning to pretend all over again.

BIRLING. Look—for God's sake!

MRS. BIRLING. (*Protesting.*) Arthur!

BIRLING. Well, my dear, they're so damned exasperating. They just won't try to understand our position or to see the difference between a lot of stuff like this coming out in private, and a downright public scandal.

ERIC. (*Shouting.* SHEILA *crosses to* L. *table.*) And I say the girl's dead and we all helped to kill her —and that's what matters ——

BIRLING. (*Also shouting, threatening* ERIC, *and crossing to him.*) And I say—either stop shouting or get out. (*Glaring at him, but in quiet tone.*) Some fathers I know would have kicked you out of the house anyhow by this time. So hold your tongue if you want to stay here.

ERIC. (*Quietly, bitterly.*) I don't give a damn now whether I stay here or not.

BIRLING. You'll stay here long enough to give me an account of that money you stole—yes, and to pay it back, too.

SHEILA. But that won't bring Eva Smith back to life, will it?

ERIC. And it doesn't alter the fact that we all helped to kill her.

GERALD. But is it a fact?

ERIC. (*Crossing to alcove.*) Of course it is. You don't know the whole story yet.

SHEILA. I suppose you're going to prove now you didn't spend last summer keeping this girl instead of seeing me, eh?

GERALD. I did keep a girl last summer. I've admitted it. And I'm sorry, Sheila.

61

SHEILA. Well, I must admit you came out of it better than the rest of us. The Inspector said that.

BIRLING. (*Angrily.*) He wasn't an inspector.

SHEILA. (*Flaring up.*) Well, he inspected us, all right! And don't let's start dodging and pretending now. Between us we drove that girl to suicide.

GERALD. Did we? Who says so? Because I say—there's no more real evidence we did than there was that that chap was a police inspector.

SHEILA. Of course there is.

GERALD. (*Steps* C.) No, there isn't. Look at it. A man comes here pretending to be a police officer. It's a hoax of some kind. Now what does he do? Very artfully working on bits of information he's picked up (ERIC *at* U. L. *table.*) here and there, he bluffs us into confessing that we've all been mixed up in this girl's life in one way or another.

ERIC. And so we have.

GERALD. But *how do you know it's the same girl?* (*Crosses to* ERIC *at table.*)

BIRLING. (*Eagerly, crossing* C.) Now wait a minute! Let's see how that would work. Now —— (*Hesitates. Crosses to fireplace.*) No, it wouldn't.

ERIC. We all admitted it.

GERALD. (*Crossing to* ERIC.) All right, you all admitted something to do with a girl. But how do you know it's the *same* girl? (*He looks around triumphantly at them. As they puzzle this out, he turns to* BIRLING, *after pause. Crosses to him.*) Look here, Mr. Birling. You sack a girl called Eva Smith. You've forgotten, but he shows you a photograph of her and then you remember. Right?

BIRLING. Yes, that part's straightforward enough. But what then?

GERALD. Well, then he happens to know that Sheila once had a girl sacked from Milward's shop. He tells us that it's this same Eva Smith. And he shows her a photograph that she remembers.

SHEILA. (*Sitting* L. *chair.*) Yes. The same photograph.

GERALD. How do you know it's the same photograph? Did you see the one your father looked at?

SHEILA. No, I didn't.

GERALD. And did he see the one the Inspector showed you?

SHEILA. No, he didn't. I see what you mean. (ERIC *crosses* D. L., *sits.*)

GERALD. We've no proof it was the same photograph and therefore no proof it was the same girl. Now take me. I never saw a photograph, remember. He caught me out by suddenly announcing that this girl changed her name to Daisy Renton. I gave myself away at once because I'd known a Daisy Renton.

BIRLING. (*Eagerly.*) And there wasn't the slightest proof that this Daisy Renton was really Eva Smith.

GERALD. Exactly.

BIRLING. We've only his word for it, and we'd his word for it that he was a police inspector and we know now he was lying. So he could have been lying all the time.

GERALD. Exactly. He probably was. Now what happened after I left? (*Sits R. chair.*)

MRS. BIRLING. (*Crossing to armchair, sits.*) I was upset because Eric had left the house, and this man said that if Eric didn't come back, he'd have to go and find him. (BIRLING *sits before fireplace.*) Well, that made me feel worse still. And his manner was so severe and he seemed so confident. Then quite suddenly he said I'd seen Eva Smith only two weeks ago.

BIRLING. Those were his exact words.

MRS. BIRLING. And like a fool, I said, Yes, I had.

BIRLING. I don't see now why you did that. She didn't call herself Eva Smith when she came to see you at the Committee, did she?

MRS. BIRLING. No, of course she didn't. And I ought to have said so. But, feeling so worried, when he suddenly turned on me with those questions, I answered more or less as he wanted me to answer.

SHEILA. But, Mother, don't forget that he showed you a photograph of the girl before that, and you obviously recognized her.

GERALD. Did anybody else see that photograph?

MRS. BIRLING. No, he showed it only to me.

GERALD. Then, don't you see, there's still no proof it was really the same girl. He might have shown you the photograph of any girl who applied to the Committee. And how do we know she was either Eva Smith or Daisy Renton?

BIRLING. Gerald's dead right. He could have used a different photograph each time, and we'd be none the wiser. We may all have been recognizing different girls?

GERALD. (*A step to* ERIC.) Exactly. Did he ask you to identify a photograph, Eric?

ERIC. No. He didn't need a photograph by the time he'd got round to me. But obviously it must have been the girl I knew who went round to see Mother.

GERALD. Why must it?

ERIC. She said she had to have help because she wouldn't take any more stolen money. And the girl I knew had already told me that.

GERALD. Even then, that may have been all nonsense.

ERIC. (*Rising.*) I don't see much nonsense about it when a girl goes and kills herself. You may be getting yourselves out nicely, but I can't. Nor can Mother. We did her in all right.

BIRLING. (*Eagerly.*) Don't be in such a hurry to put yourself into court. That interview with your mother could have been just as much a put-up job, like all this police inspector business. The whole damned thing can have been a piece of bluff.

ERIC. (*Angrily.*) How can it? The girl's dead, isn't she?

GERALD. But what girl? There were probably four or five different girls.

ERIC. That doesn't matter to me. The one I knew is dead.

BIRLING. Is she? *How do we know she is?*

GERALD. That's right. You've got it. How do we know any girl killed herself today?

BIRLING. (*Looking at them triumphantly.*) Now answer that one.

ERIC. But—look here—it all began with that.

BIRLING. That doesn't mean it's true.

GERALD. As a matter of fact, it didn't begin with that. It began with this fellow announcing himself as a police inspector. And we know now that he wasn't—just somebody hoaxing us.

SHEILA. I see what you mean. But for all that I wouldn't be too sure about the hoaxing part. He didn't look like a hoaxer to me. (*Rises, crossing above L. chair.*)

BIRLING. Of course he didn't. Otherwise, he'd have been wasting his time. He had to give an impressive performance.

MRS. BIRLING. It didn't deceive me.

BIRLING. (*Crossing D. R.*) Well—perhaps not. But look at it from his point of view. We're having a little celebration here and feeling rather pleased with ourselves. Now he has to work this trick on us. Well, the first thing he has to do is to give us such a shock that after that he can bluff us all the time. So he starts right off. A girl has just died in the Infirmary. She drank some strong disinfectant. Died in agony ——

64

ERIC. All right, don't pile it on.

BIRLING. (*Triumphantly.*) There you are, you see. Just repeating it shakes you a bit. And that's what he had to do. Shake us at once—and then start questioning us—until we didn't know where we were. Oh—let's admit that. He took us all right. He had the laugh on us.

ERIC. He could laugh his head off—if I knew it really was all a hoax.

BIRLING. I'm convinced it is. No police inquiry. No one girl that all this happened to. No scandal ——

SHEILA. (*Sits L.*) And no suicide?

GERALD. (*Decisively. Rises.*) We can settle that at once.

SHEILA. How?

GERALD. By calling up the Infirmary. Either there's a dead girl there or there isn't.

BIRLING. (*Uneasily. Rises.*) It 'ud look a bit queer, wouldn't it— ringing up at this time of night ——

GERALD. (*Crossing D. R.*) I don't mind doing it. Mind you, they may have a girl there who committed suicide, and that may have given this fellow the idea of coming here and frightening us. But even if there is, we've no way of knowing if it's the one who's been talked about tonight.

MRS. BIRLING. (*Emphatically.*) And if there isn't ——

GERALD. Then obviously that's the final and definite proof that the whole thing is a sell. And now we'll see. (*He goes to telephone and looks up number. Others watch tensely.*) Brumley eight-nine-eight-six. . . . Is that the Infirmary? This is Mr. Gerald Croft— of Crofts Limited . . . yes. . . . We're rather worried about one of our employees. Have you had a girl brought in this afternoon who committed suicide by drinking disinfectant—or any suicide? . . . (SHEILA *rises—all step in.*) Yes, I'll wait. (*As he waits, others show their nervous tension.* BIRLING *wipes his brow.* SHEILA *shivers,* ERIC *clasps and unclasps his hands, etc.*) Yes? . . . You're certain of that. . . . I see. . . . Well, thank you very much. Good night. (*Puts down receiver and looks at them.*) No girl has died in there today. No girl's been brought in after drinking disinfectant. They haven't had a suicide for months.

BIRLING. (*Triumphantly. Crosses to R. chair.*) There you are! Proof positively. The whole story's just a lot of moonshine. Nothing but an elaborate sell! (*Produces a huge sigh of relief.*) No-

body likes to be sold as badly as that—but—for all that ——
(*Smiles at them all.*) What a relief! Gerald, a drink.

GERALD. (*Smiling.*) Thanks, I think I could just do with one now.

BIRLING. (*Crossing to alcove and going to sideboard.*) So could I

MRS. BIRLING. (*Smiling.*) And I must say, Gerald, you've argued this very cleverly, and I'm most grateful.

GERALD. (*Going for his drink.*) Well, you see, while I was out for a walk I'd time to cool off and think things out a little.

BIRLING. (*Giving him drink. Crosses down R. C.—GERALD to U. L. table.*) Yes, he didn't keep you on the run as he did the rest of us. I'll admit now he gave me a bit of a scare at the time. But I'd a special reason for not wanting any public scandal just now. (*Has his drink now, and raises glass. GERALD sits in R. chair.*) Well, here's to us. Come on, Sheila, don't look like that. All over now.

SHEILA. (*Slowly.*) The worst part is. But you're forgetting one thing I still can't forget. Everything we said had happened really had happened. If it didn't end tragically, then that's lucky for us. But it might have done.

BIRLING. (*Jovially.*) But the whole thing's different now. Come, come, you can see that, can't you? (*Imitating* INSPECTOR *in his final speech.*) *You all helped to kill her.* (*Pointing at* SHEILA *and* ERIC *and laughing.*) And I wish you could have seen the look on your faces when he said that. And the artful devil knew all the time nobody had died and the whole story was bunkum. Oh, he was clever. But he who laughs last—whatever it is. (*Sits R. chair.* SHEILA *moves toward door.*) Going to bed, young woman?

SHEILA. (*Tensely.*) I want to get out of this. It frightens me the way you talk.

BIRLING. (*Heartily.*) Nonsense! You'll have a good laugh over it yet. Fellow comes here and starts inventing ——

SHEILA. He didn't invent what each of us admitted to doing—did he?

BIRLING. Well, what if he didn't? Look, you'd better ask Gerald for that ring you gave back to him, hadn't you? Then you'll feel better.

SHEILA. (*Passionately.*) You're pretending everything's just as it was before!

ERIC. I'm not!

SHEILA. No, but these others are.

BIRLING. Well, isn't it? We've been had, that's all.

SHEILA. So nothing really happened! So there's nothing to be sorry for, nothing to learn. We can all go on behaving just as we did.

MRS. BIRLING. Well, why shouldn't we?

SHEILA. I tell you—whoever that Inspector was, it was anything but a joke. You knew it then. You began to learn something. And now you've stopped. You're ready to go on in the same old way.

BIRLING. (*Amused.*) And you're not, eh?

SHEILA. No, because I remember what he said, how he looked, and what he made me feel. And it frightens me the way you talk, and I can't listen to any more of it. (GERALD *rises, crosses to her.*)

BIRLING. Well, go to bed then, and don't stand there being hysterical.

MRS. BIRLING. She's over-tired. In the morning she'll be as amused as we are.

GERALD. Everything's all right now, Sheila. (*Holds up engagement ring.*) What about this ring?

SHEILA. No, not yet. It's too soon. I must think.

BIRLING. (*Pointing to* ERIC *and* SHEILA.) Now look at the pair of them—the famous younger generation who know it all. And they can't even take a joke —— (*Telephone rings sharply. A moment's complete silence.* BIRLING *goes to answer it.*) Yes? . . . Mr. Birling speaking. . . . *What?*—Here —— (*But obviously the other person has rung off. He puts telephone down slowly and looks in a panic-stricken fashion at others.*) That was the police. A girl has just died—on her way to the Infirmary—after swallowing some disinfectant. And a Police Inspector is on his way here—to ask some—questions —— (*As they stare guiltily and dumbfounded.* SHEILA *faces door. As she rises—*)

THE CURTAIN FALLS SLOWLY

PROPERTY LIST

Dessert plates, champagne glasses and empty bottle
Decanter of port, port glasses, cigarette box with cigarettes, matches
Tray for dishes
Ring case (small box with engagement ring in it)
Cigars
Small photo (unframed)
Whisky and glasses
Watch
Notebook and pencil
Phone book

NEW PLAYS

★ **GUARDIANS by Peter Morris.** In this unflinching look at war, a disgraced American soldier discloses the truth about Abu Ghraib prison, and a clever English journalist reveals how he faked a similar story for the London tabloids. "Compelling, sympathetic and powerful." *—NY Times.* "Sends you into a state of moral turbulence." *—Sunday Times (UK).* "Nothing short of remarkable." *—Village Voice.* [1M, 1W] ISBN: 978-0-8222-2177-7

★ **BLUE DOOR by Tanya Barfield.** Three generations of men (all played by one actor), from slavery through Black Power, challenge Lewis, a tenured professor of mathematics, to embark on a journey combining past and present. "A teasing flare for words." *—Village Voice.* "Unfailingly thought-provoking." *—LA Times.* "The play moves with the speed and logic of a dream." *—Seattle Weekly.* [2M] ISBN: 978-0-8222-2209-5

★ **THE INTELLIGENT DESIGN OF JENNY CHOW by Rolin Jones.** This irreverent "techno-comedy" chronicles one brilliant woman's quest to determine her heritage and face her fears with the help of her astounding creation called Jenny Chow. "Boldly imagined." *—NY Times.* "Fantastical and funny." *—Variety.* "Harvests many laughs and finally a few tears." *—LA Times.* [3M, 3W] ISBN: 978-0-8222-2071-8

★ **SOUVENIR by Stephen Temperley.** Florence Foster Jenkins, a wealthy society eccentric, suffers under the delusion that she is a great coloratura soprano—when in fact the opposite is true. "Hilarious and deeply touching. Incredibly moving and breathtaking." *—NY Daily News.* "A sweet love letter of a play." *—NY Times.* "Wildly funny. Completely charming." *—Star-Ledger.* [1M, 1W] ISBN: 978-0-8222-2157-9

★ **ICE GLEN by Joan Ackermann.** In this touching period comedy, a beautiful poetess dwells in idyllic obscurity on a Berkshire estate with a band of unlikely cohorts. "A beautifully written story of nature and change." *—Talkin' Broadway.* "A lovely play which will leave you with a lot to think about." *—CurtainUp.* "Funny, moving and witty." *—Metroland (Boston).* [4M, 3W] ISBN: 978-0-8222-2175-3

★ **THE LAST DAYS OF JUDAS ISCARIOT by Stephen Adly Guirgis.** Set in a time-bending, darkly comic world between heaven and hell, this play reexamines the plight and fate of the New Testament's most infamous sinner. "An unforced eloquence that finds the poetry in lowdown street talk." *—NY Times.* "A real jaw-dropper." *—Variety.* "An extraordinary play." *—Guardian (UK).* [10M, 5W] ISBN: 978-0-8222-2082-4

DRAMATISTS PLAY SERVICE, INC.
440 Park Avenue South, New York, NY 10016 212-683-8960 Fax 212-213-1539
postmaster@dramatists.com www.dramatists.com

NEW PLAYS

★ THE GREAT AMERICAN TRAILER PARK MUSICAL music and lyrics by David Nehls, book by Betsy Kelso. Pippi, a stripper on the run, has just moved into Armadillo Acres, wreaking havoc among the tenants of Florida's most exclusive trailer park. "Adultery, strippers, murderous ex-boyfriends, Costco and the Ice Capades. Undeniable fun." –*NY Post.* "Joyful and unashamedly vulgar." –*The New Yorker.* "Sparkles with treasure." –*New York Sun.* [2M, 5W] ISBN: 978-0-8222-2137-1

★ MATCH by Stephen Belber. When a young Seattle couple meet a prominent New York choreographer, they are led on a fraught journey that will change their lives forever. "Uproariously funny, deeply moving, enthralling theatre." –*NY Daily News.* "Prolific laughs and ear-to-ear smiles." –*NY Magazine.* [2M, 1W] ISBN: 978-0-8222-2020-6

★ MR. MARMALADE by Noah Haidle. Four-year-old Lucy's imaginary friend, Mr. Marmalade, doesn't have much time for her—not to mention he has a cocaine addiction and a penchant for pornography. "Alternately hilarious and heartbreaking." –*The New Yorker.* "A mature and accomplished play." –*LA Times.* "Scathingly observant comedy." –*Miami Herald.* [4M, 2W] ISBN: 978-0-8222-2142-5

★ MOONLIGHT AND MAGNOLIAS by Ron Hutchinson. Three men cloister themselves as they work tirelessly to reshape a screenplay that's just not working—*Gone with the Wind.* "Consumers of vintage Hollywood insider stories will eat up Hutchinson's diverting conjecture." –*Variety.* "A lot of fun." –*NY Post.* "A Hollywood dream-factory farce." –*Chicago Sun-Times.* [3M, 1W] ISBN: 978-0-8222-2084-8

★ THE LEARNED LADIES OF PARK AVENUE by David Grimm, translated and freely adapted from Molière's *Les Femmes Savantes.* Dicky wants to marry Betty, but her mother's plan is for Betty to wed a most pompous man. "A brave, brainy and barmy revision." –*Hartford Courant.* "A rare but welcome bird in contemporary theatre." –*New Haven Register.* "Roll over Cole Porter." –*Boston Globe.* [5M, 5W] ISBN: 978-0-8222-2135-7

★ REGRETS ONLY by Paul Rudnick. A sparkling comedy of Manhattan manners that explores the latest topics in marriage, friendships and squandered riches. "One of the funniest quip-meisters on the planet." –*NY Times.* "Precious moments of hilarity. Devastatingly accurate political and social satire." –*BackStage.* "Great fun." –*CurtainUp.* [3M, 3W] ISBN: 978-0-8222-2223-1

DRAMATISTS PLAY SERVICE, INC.
440 Park Avenue South, New York, NY 10016 212-683-8960 Fax 212-213-1539
postmaster@dramatists.com   www.dramatists.com

NEW PLAYS

★ **AFTER ASHLEY by Gina Gionfriddo.** A teenager is unwillingly thrust into the national spotlight when a family tragedy becomes talk-show fodder. "A work that virtually any audience would find accessible." –*NY Times.* "Deft characterization and caustic humor." –*NY Sun.* "A smart satirical drama." –*Variety.* [4M, 2W] ISBN: 978-0-8222-2099-2

★ **THE RUBY SUNRISE by Rinne Groff.** Twenty-five years after Ruby struggles to realize her dream of inventing the first television, her daughter faces similar battles of faith as she works to get Ruby's story told on network TV. "Measured and intelligent, optimistic yet clear-eyed." –*NY Magazine.* "Maintains an exciting sense of ingenuity." –*Village Voice.* "Sinuous theatrical flair." –*Broadway.com.* [3M, 4W] ISBN: 978-0-8222-2140-1

★ **MY NAME IS RACHEL CORRIE taken from the writings of Rachel Corrie, edited by Alan Rickman and Katharine Viner.** This solo piece tells the story of Rachel Corrie who was killed in Gaza by an Israeli bulldozer set to demolish a Palestinian home. "Heartbreaking urgency. An invigoratingly detailed portrait of a passionate idealist." –*NY Times.* "Deeply authentically human." –*USA Today.* "A stunning dramatization." –*CurtainUp.* [1W] ISBN: 978-0-8222-2222-4

★ **ALMOST, MAINE by John Cariani.** This charming midwinter night's dream of a play turns romantic clichés on their ear as it chronicles the painfully hilarious amorous adventures (and misadventures) of residents of a remote northern town that doesn't quite exist. "A whimsical approach to the joys and perils of romance." –*NY Times.* "Sweet, poignant and witty." –*NY Daily News.* "Aims for the heart by way of the funny bone." –*Star-Ledger.* [2M, 2W] ISBN: 978-0-8222-2156-2

★ **Mitch Albom's TUESDAYS WITH MORRIE by Jeffrey Hatcher and Mitch Albom, based on the book by Mitch Albom.** The true story of Brandeis University professor Morrie Schwartz and his relationship with his student Mitch Albom. "A touching, life-affirming, deeply emotional drama." –*NY Daily News.* "You'll laugh. You'll cry." –*Variety.* "Moving and powerful." –*NY Post.* [2M] ISBN: 978-0-8222-2188-3

★ **DOG SEES GOD: CONFESSIONS OF A TEENAGE BLOCKHEAD by Bert V. Royal.** An abused pianist and a pyromaniac ex-girlfriend contribute to the teen-angst of America's most hapless kid. "A welcome antidote to the notion that the *Peanuts* gang provides merely American cuteness." –*NY Times.* "Hysterically funny." –*NY Post.* "The *Peanuts* kids have finally come out of their shells." –*Time Out.* [4M, 4W] ISBN: 978-0-8222-2152-4

DRAMATISTS PLAY SERVICE, INC.
440 Park Avenue South, New York, NY 10016 212-683-8960 Fax 212-213-1539
postmaster@dramatists.com www.dramatists.com

NEW PLAYS

★ **RABBIT HOLE by David Lindsay-Abaire.** Winner of the 2007 Pulitzer Prize. Becca and Howie Corbett have everything a couple could want until a life-shattering accident turns their world upside down. "An intensely emotional examination of grief, laced with wit." —*Variety.* "A transcendent and deeply affecting new play." —*Entertainment Weekly.* "Painstakingly beautiful." —*BackStage.* [2M, 3W] ISBN: 978-0-8222-2154-8

★ **DOUBT, A Parable by John Patrick Shanley.** Winner of the 2005 Pulitzer Prize and Tony Award. Sister Aloysius, a Bronx school principal, takes matters into her own hands when she suspects the young Father Flynn of improper relations with one of the male students. "All the elements come invigoratingly together like clockwork." —*Variety.* "Passionate, exquisite, important, engrossing." —*NY Newsday.* [1M, 3W] ISBN: 978-0-8222-2219-4

★ **THE PILLOWMAN by Martin McDonagh.** In an unnamed totalitarian state, an author of horrific children's stories discovers that someone has been making his stories come true. "A blindingly bright black comedy." —*NY Times.* "McDonagh's least forgiving, bravest play." —*Variety.* "Thoroughly startling and genuinely intimidating." —*Chicago Tribune.* [4M, 5 bit parts (2M, 1W, 1 boy, 1 girl)] ISBN: 978-0-8222-2100-5

★ **GREY GARDENS book by Doug Wright, music by Scott Frankel, lyrics by Michael Korie.** The hilarious and heartbreaking story of Big Edie and Little Edie Bouvier Beale, the eccentric aunt and cousin of Jacqueline Kennedy Onassis, once bright names on the social register who became East Hampton's most notorious recluses. "An experience no passionate theatergoer should miss." —*NY Times.* "A unique and unmissable musical." —*Rolling Stone.* [4M, 3W, 2 girls] ISBN: 978-0-8222-2181-4

★ **THE LITTLE DOG LAUGHED by Douglas Carter Beane.** Mitchell Green could make it big as the hot new leading man in Hollywood if Diane, his agent, could just keep him in the closet. "Devastatingly funny." —*NY Times.* "An out-and-out delight." —*NY Daily News.* "Full of wit and wisdom." —*NY Post.* [2M, 2W] ISBN: 978-0-8222-2226-2

★ **SHINING CITY by Conor McPherson.** A guilt-ridden man reaches out to a therapist after seeing the ghost of his recently deceased wife. "Haunting, inspired and glorious." —*NY Times.* "Simply breathtaking and astonishing." —*Time Out.* "A thoughtful, artful, absorbing new drama." —*Star-Ledger.* [3M, 1W] ISBN: 978-0-8222-2187-6

DRAMATISTS PLAY SERVICE, INC.
440 Park Avenue South, New York, NY 10016 212-683-8960 Fax 212-213-1539
postmaster@dramatists.com www.dramatists.com